A GUIDE TO
SKY MONSTERS

A GUIDE TO
SKY MONSTERS

**Thunderbirds, the Jersey Devil, Mothman,
and Other Flying Cryptids**

T. S. Mart and Mel Cabre
Illustrations by Mel Cabre

RED ⚡ LIGHTNING BOOKS

This book is a publication of

Red Lightning Books
1320 East 10th Street
Bloomington, Indiana 47405 USA

redlightningbooks.com

First paperback edition 2023
© 2021 by T. S. Mart and Mel Cabre

Manufactured in the United States of America

First printing 2023

ISBN 978-1-68435-217-3

To my grandpa, James Ayers
You taught me to soar beyond the sky's limit.

—*Mel Cabre*

To Tony and Denise
Your unconditional support means the world to me.

—*T. S. Mart*

CONTENTS

PREFACE

Maybe it's the writer in me . . . or the social worker, but I have always been intrigued by human behavior. Even as a young child, I analyzed family, friends, and even strangers, trying to figure out how some people were successful and others not so much. I knew if I could avoid the mistakes they made, my life would be perfect.

The problem with my theory was no matter how I prepared, I had no clue how I would react to change until I was ankle deep in it. No two people react the same because life variables train us to look at the world through slightly different lenses. The most important variable is our belief system (not believing in something is also a belief system). Our belief system figures into every facet of our life.

What does this have to do with Sky Monsters—those cryptids that fly? More than you might realize. More than I realized. Cryptids that rise out of the sentiments of the times often have deep historical or cultural roots. This couldn't be more true for the Thunderbird, Jersey Devil, and Mothman.

Not only were belief systems at play during the rise of these cryptids but so were the nasty seeds of intolerance and distrust. What we believe + high emotion = volatile reactions. Unchecked, this combination becomes a breeding ground for hate—even in the world of cryptids. But why? We're talking about unknown animals or creatures. These were my thoughts as I read through many books, articles, and websites.

Conversely, for every serious side of a cryptid there is also a fun and fantastical side. Mel—the heart and soul behind our cryptid projects—brings the fun. She has profiled over thirty-five unknown flying cryptids and illustrated many of them. Without her talent and imagination, this book wouldn't be possible. Because of our blending talents, this book may be different from other cryptid books, but we hope it offers you a comprehensive look at the world of flying cryptids. Thank you for reading.

—*T.S. Mart*

ACKNOWLEDGMENTS

FIRST AND FOREMOST, WE WOULD LIKE TO THANK our families who put up with our isolation while we're in the middle of a project. For those of you who support and believe in us—it means the world.

We're always grateful for the real experts in the field: cryptozoologists like Loren Coleman, Ken Gerhard, Mark A. Hall, David Weatherly, Johnathan Whitcomb, Paul Nation, and the guys at Genesis Park, who understand the field of flying cryptids so much better than we do.

Thank you to Bill Iseminger and the Cahokia Mounds State Historic Site for reading and helping with the Piasa Monster portion of this book.

We'd also like to thank the crew at Indiana University Press for being patient as we finalized this book. To editors, Ashley Runyon and Anna Francis, thank you for believing in this project. Thank you, Nancy Lightfoot and the copy editors. I stand in awe of your knowledge and eagle eye gift. This book shines because of you. Thank you to all the project managers; design team; and marketing. We appreciate you and all that you do make each project a success.

A GUIDE TO
SKY MONSTERS

1

WHAT ARE SKY MONSTERS?

The World of Flying Monsters

Sky monsters. Flying cryptids. Unknown creatures that haunt the heights of our world. Maybe you've never heard of them, or possibly you have and fully understand how these cryptids have crept their way into our culture and stirred up controversy, terrorized communities, impacted national pride, and showed the world how intolerance degrades our quality of life.

The Thunderbird, the Jersey Devil, Mothman. These aren't just modern monsters meant to satisfy curious minds looking for answers. From each of these cryptids emerges a legacy of lives that have been shaken and belief systems challenged. Their origins and what they symbolize remind us of where we have traveled and where we dare not go again.

Giants in the world of unknown flying creatures, these three have been the subject of multiple books and movies that detail their existence in various genres and from various points of view. They're each unique. We'll discuss how later on, but it's important to note up front that each of these fliers emerged, in widely varying circumstances, to satisfy one (or more) of three distinct needs within their local communities.

- The need for answers to life's mysteries
- The need to cast blame or maintain control
- The need to justify or be right

These are universal needs everyone experiences from time to time. That is why the stories surrounding sky cryptids are timeless and compelling. By examining how each came into existence—through unanswered questions, the pain associated with loss, or lies or egos that colored the times—we can better understand ourselves, our belief systems, and our worldviews.

Thunderbird depictions may vary across cultures and periods of time because people observed different creatures in the sky. While terrifying, a bird or flying reptile of enormous size demands respect. Early people passed on what they perceived as life and death encounters to teach, remember, and entertain.

The Thunderbird category is broad and can refer to different creatures depending on history and context. Regardless, each flying creature is a unique species that once existed, if only in spiritual teachings, in the imaginations of witnesses, or in the lives they changed. While those listed below may not include every Thunderbird discussed throughout history, we'll cover some of the most popular, starting with the fossil record.

Pterodactyloidea—Winged Fingers

Quetzalcoatlus

This flying or gliding reptile was approximately eighteen feet tall with a wingspan nearing thirty-six feet, and scientists believe it weighed 300 to 550 pounds. The combined length of its legs and feet was nearly seven feet.

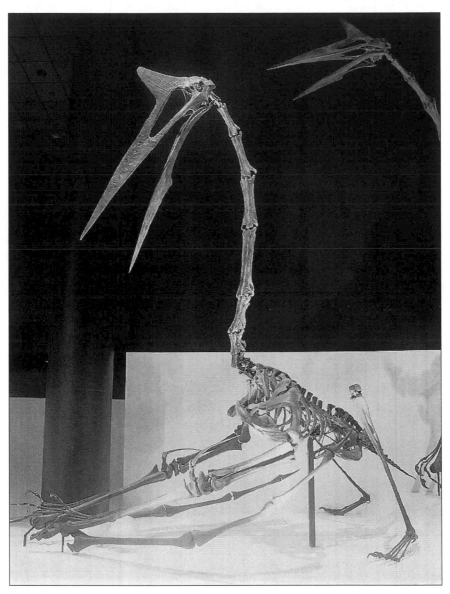

Quetzalcoatlus fossil at the Houston Museum of Natural Science.
Photo credit: Yinan Chen. Public Domain.

Quetzalcoatlus is believed to have been primarily terrestrial, but its hollow bones and light-weight wings would have permitted it to soar off cliffs and glide for significant distances. *Quetzalcoatlus* could have easily preyed on small dinosaurs, animals, and some believe even humans—and assume they coexisted. There are varying opinions on this topic, which we'll cover in more detail in chapter 4.

The first *Quetzalcoatlus* fossil was discovered and recorded in 1971 by graduate student Douglas Lawson in Texas's Big Bend National Park. In 1975, scientists named the reptile after the Aztec god Quetzalcoatl, the patron god of the priesthood of learning and knowledge. *Quetzalcoatlus* means "feathered serpent." We can't know whether pre-Columbian peoples of North America witnessed *Quetzalcoatlus* in action, but a likeness of a large-winged, five-toed creature appears in some of their pottery and artwork.

Pteranodons

A smaller cousin of the *Quetzalcoatlus*, the *Pteranodon*, is also a member of the Pterodactyloidea suborder. It stood nearly six feet tall and was believed to weigh about fifty pounds—still a good size for a bird. *Pteranodon* means "toothless wing," but it's speculated the fliers were carnivorous. O. C. Marsh discovered this flying reptile in 1870 in the chalk beds of Kansas and Nebraska and across the Great Plains of North America. The chalk beds were once an inland sea, so *Pteranodons* likely lived on a diet of fish. Paleontologists also found fearsome-looking skeletons of mosasaurs in the chalk beds that may have feasted on water-skimming *Pteranodons*—much like a scene out of *Jurassic World*, only on a smaller scale.

Dinosaurs, mosasaurs, and other extinct marine life were fossilized alongside *Pteranodon* when a catastrophic event buried them together. *Pteranodons* are also assumed to be extinct, but is it possible some *Pteranodons* escaped because they could fly away from disaster? Perhaps the flying reptiles fed off the inland sea until it dried up then migrated south. Could this account for the frightful man-eating-bird stories told by the indigenous people of southwestern North America? Is it possible that man coexisted with the surviving *Pteranodons* and hunted the flying reptiles to extinction . . . or near extinction?

Modern day *Pteranodon* sightings have been reported in several American states and around the world, but either these sky reptiles have kept their distance from humans or witnesses have been afraid to share their photos and videos. History has proven that sharing the strange and unusual often results in disbelief and derision.

Cathartiformes

Teratorns

The fossilized remains of over one hundred *Teratornis merriami* have been recovered from the sticky tar of Rancho La Brea in Southern California. Also known as Merriam's Teratorn, this particular bird is a distant relative of the California Condor. But with a wingspan of around twelve feet and weighing about thirty-three pounds, the teratorn beats out even the larger Andean condor, which is the closest living bird in terms of size.

Teratorn means "wonder bird" in Greek. John C. Merriam and Loye Miller, American paleontologists who served as professors of zoology at the University of California, discovered the first remains in the early 1900s. Miller named the species in 1909. There is a larger teratorn previously known as *Teratornis incredibilis*. In light of taxonomic changes, they now classify this enormous bird as *Aiolornis incredibilis*. This reptile carried a wingspan of approximately sixteen to eighteen feet.

Because the teratorns' skulls are shaped differently than the condors, scientists believe it was primarily a predator, but in his book *Extinct Animals*, Ross Piper suggests that scavenging was also an important part of the Teratorns' diet: "Although Merriam's Teratorn may have had a similar lifestyle to the living bald eagle, it must have been heavily dependent on carrion, particularly the carcasses of large mammals, as its demise coincides with the disappearance of the large North American animals. With suitable carcasses becoming scarcer and scarcer and humans hunting them for food, the long-lived but slow-breeding Merriam's Teratorn was doomed, and sadly, it died out."[1]

But what if teratorns aren't extinct? Is it possible these magnificent fliers are the thunderbirds revered by Native Americans and still seen flying overhead by witnesses today? Perhaps remnant populations of these birds still exist in remote areas. Is it possible that individuals wander into the skies over human habitation and, confused, mistake children and livestock for prey?

Thunderbirds

Representing courage, strength, and power, the Thunderbird has become a pop-culture icon in the United States. Feared and respected, this greatest-of-all weather spirits appears in many Native American mythologies and is said to bring life and death as it follows weather patterns across the skies. Legend says a thunderous noise shakes the air when it flaps its enormous wings, and lightning shoots from its eyes as it roams the earth, seeking to nurture and sometimes to destroy. The Thunderbird is considered to be a protector of the people in diverse cultures. According to Algonquian legend, Thunderbird is constantly at war with the destructive water serpent, and many natural phenomena are considered to be the results of their battles.

Native Americans perceive thunderbirds to be not exactly animal or human but a combination of both, and this spiritual duality allows man to assume Thunderbird characteristics. But do thunderbirds exist as animals? Eyewitness accounts dating back to the mid-1800s report this giant bird soaring high overhead during the day, often near water and heavily forested areas. It's unknown how these creatures relate to the birdlike deity of Native American cultures, but there are midwestern tribes around the Great Lakes who celebrated great birds who brought the spring rains, observed the birds' behaviors, and recorded their nesting sites.

Most witnesses who report seeing thunderbirds describe them as black or brown to dark gray, with a wingspan of twelve to twenty feet. (For perspective, the Bald Eagle's wingspan ranges from six to seven-and-a-half feet.) Thunderbirds are thought to be opportunistic birds of prey that feast on large and small game—including humans—and occasionally dead animals. Some say they have white rings around their necks, white on the tips of their wings, and black or yellow beaks, but descriptions vary. In 1954, just

south of the Olympic Peninsula in Oregon, onlookers spotted several giant birds they said looked like airplanes. The *Oakland Tribune*, in 1975, told of a Walnut Creek resident who looked into his backyard to see a five-foot tall bird take flight, spreading its wings as wide as fifteen feet.[2]

FUN FACT: With a wingspan of nearly ten feet, the California condor is the largest known flying bird in the United States. They inhabit the forests, rocky shrublands, and oak savannas of California, Arizona, and Utah. The Wandering Albatross of Antarctica has the largest wingspan of any known bird at twelve feet.

Many sightings of large birds have taken place in and around Illinois. In the first half of 1948, sightings of grayish-green birds about the size of a piper cub were seen near Alton, Illinois, and St. Louis, Missouri. Witnesses thought they were looking at an airplane until the bird flapped its wings. In 1968, birds with wingspans ranging between fifteen and twenty feet were spotted around Galesburg, Illinois. Then in 1977, a mother reported to police that a giant bird carried her boy about thirty or forty feet across the yard before dropping him to the ground. These "Lawndale Monsters" (there were two birds) flew north toward a nearby creek. A second witness observed the birds taking off and said they sounded like a jet on takeoff but were silent during flight. When wildlife officials brought pictures of birds that might have carried off a child for the boy's mother to look at, she could not identify them, stating the birds she had seen were unlike any known species in the area.

Other reported sightings of these enormous birds surfaced the same year, but the story quickly died out when the Associated Press circulated an article that reported the birds had been identified as vultures. One disillusioned ten-year-old witness and his family refused to talk any further about it.

A conglomeration of many wooded areas, the Black Forest of northern Pennsylvania encompasses Cameron, Clinton, Elk, Lycoming, McKean, Potter, Tioga, and Warren Counties and is home to the greatest number of thunderbird sightings. In fact, studies by cryptozoologists reveal a pattern in historical reports in the area that show "the birds engaging in a seasonal migration, southward in the winter and northward in the warmer months."[3]

In *Thunderbirds: America's Living Legends of Giant Birds* (2004), Mark Hall shares the reports of the late Robert Lyman Sr., who recorded thunderbird sightings from 1890 up until the 1970s. Witness testimonies include those who say they saw the birds carrying fawns or roadkill or simply flying overhead. In 1973, one couple reported a large black bird standing alongside the road. As they approached, the bird spread its massive wings and flapped them slowly and heavily, struggling to get off the ground. As it rose above the car, one wing slapped the windshield, scaring the couple. Then it gained more height and disappeared above the trees.

Hall also writes about Pennsylvania resident Hiram Cranmer, who reported his sightings to *Fate Magazine*, popularizing the bird's presence in the state. Detailed encounters of birds devouring men and abducting children instilled equal parts fear of and fascination with these mysterious creatures.

The Jersey Devil—America's Original Cryptid

Folklore surrounding the Jersey Devil dates back over 250 years to a time of early American settlements on the northeast edge of the New Jersey Pine Barrens. Not too far from Philadelphia—the hub of Quaker progress—the monster entered the scene as a demonic incarnation of an inconspicuous barrel maker from England named Daniel Leeds.

Leeds dreamed of becoming his best self while encouraging others to do the same. Ahead of his time in his thinking and definitely in the wrong place, he published the *American Almanac*, which included predictions on weather and health based on astrological formulas. Fearful that this school of thought would corrupt the community, Quaker leaders forbid him to publish. A battle of ideas erupted, turning men against one another. Slander and suppression are said to have crushed Daniel's dreams and fueled the emergence of the underlying monster who rebelled against his Quaker religion and the people he'd once called brothers.

Leeds himself eventually faded into the fine print of surveyor's documents, land deeds, and gerontological records, but the story of the Leeds Devil never lost steam. We'll discuss more about Daniel Leeds and theories of the origin of the Leeds Devil later, but a combination of local stories, prejudices, and rumors maintained belief in the monstrous figure known only to the residents of Pine Barrens. That is until 1859.

Bog iron ore and glassmaking brought industry to the Pine Barrens. The area thrived until scientists found coal and a higher quality of iron in Pennsylvania. As iron furnaces in New Jersey closed, people moved on. Those who loved the remote area stayed and lived off the land's natural resources. The vast miles of remote forest so near Philadelphia, New York, and other large cities also enticed poachers, moonshiners, and bandits to take up residence. It didn't take long for newcomers to label the locals "Pineys" and dismiss them as an uneducated, primitive, and superstitious people.

To learn more about the secluded way of life in the Pine Barrens, New York journalist, W. F. Mayer toured the region in 1858. A year later, he recorded the first written account of the Leeds Devil in the *Atlantic Monthly*. Apparently, during his visit in the Pine Barrens, a storm was moving toward them, and he quoted a woman who had said, "[This storm] will be like the one the night I seed the Leeds Devil." Standing nearby, a local man told

Mayer the story of the Leeds Devil. The man said that in 1735, Mother Leeds gave birth to a dragon-like creature that haunts the area. "Little children did be eaten and maids abused."[4]

No further written accounts appeared until the late 1800s, when rumors emerged of a distraught mother who had cursed her child while giving birth saying, "Let it be the devil." The unwanted infant is said to have morphed into a hideous creature and flown out into the night. In an 1893 article in the *New York Sun*, a railroad engineer claimed a monkey-faced Leeds Devil attacked his train.[5] In the early 1900s, Francis Bazely Lee (1869–1914), a clerk for the New Jersey Supreme Court, began compiling Leeds Devil sightings and stories while working on genealogical records. He kept the information separate and to himself, but in 1905, John Elfreth Watkins, an acquaintance of Lee's, published some of his findings in an article he called, "Demon of the Pines."[6] That same year, Watkins published a different story that claimed Mother Leeds was a witch, her husband the devil, and their child dragon-like.

These stories came on the heels of *American Myths and Legends* (1903), a book by Charles Montgomery Skinner, who offered the classic Leeds Devil description in his book. He wrote that Mother Leeds was a Quaker and a witch who gave birth to a creature with wings like a bat and feet like a pig. Another writer, Arminius Alba, wrote an article for the *Trenton Times* in 1905 that described a monkey-like creature who lived with the family for several years before flying up the chimney. This version included a Captain Leeds and his wife, who was a local gossip and sorceress. These stories paved the way for the creature's major media appearance.

During the week of January 16–23, 1909, thousands of people reported sightings of the Leeds devil or his footprints throughout the Delaware Valley area. In Bristol, Pennsylvania, a man awakened in the middle of the night to strange noises. When he looked outside, he saw a large creature with wings hopping along the towpath of the canal. The chief of police also said he saw something that looked like a hopping bird, and it screeched loudly. Others said it looked like a ram with curled horns and had long, thin wings and short front legs.

The next day, outside of Burlington, locals found hoofprints in the snow throughout the town and surrounding countryside. One woman said a cow with wings made them. A couple of days later in Gloucester city, a couple watched a creature moving about on the roof of their shed. They described it as being three and a half feet tall with the head of a collie, the face of a horse, and a long neck. It stood on stilt-like legs with horselike hooves and had a wingspan of about two feet. The front legs were short, with paws.

Later that same week, residents in Camden saw the creature at about two o'clock in the morning. A trolley was passing through Haddon Heights when passengers noticed the creature flying overhead. When the trolley stopped to pick up a passenger, the hovering creature hissed and flew away. Witnesses stated it resembled a kangaroo with a long neck and long wings, and had a dark, slender body.[7]

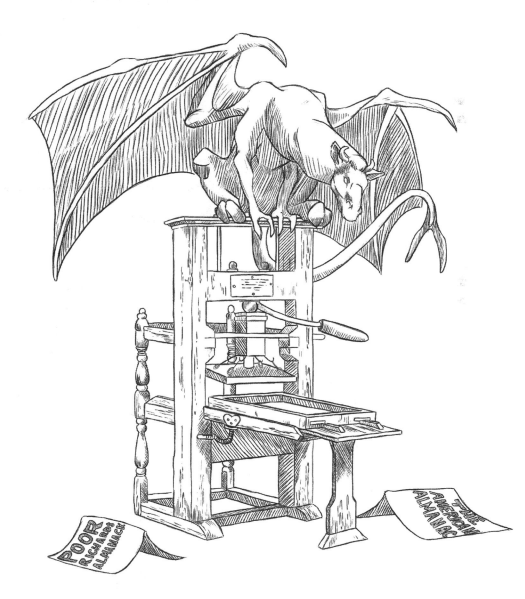

While it's difficult to pinpoint the exact moment the Leeds Devil became known as the Jersey Devil, the change happened sometime in the early twentieth century. The January 22, 1909, *Evening World Paper* printed an article titled, "Jersey's Devil Is Classified as a Bombat." In the mid-twentieth century, New Jersey journalist, amateur historian, and folklorist Henry C. Beck (1902–1965) entered the Pine Barrens to write about New Jersey people and their lives. It was during his second visit to South Jersey around 1940 that he came upon a version of the Leeds Devil story, in which a mother gives birth to a deformed child and hides it away. Beck wasn't fond of this melancholy version, and in *Jersey Genesis* (1945), his celebratory book about the region, he instead shares stories similar to those provided by W. F. Mayer and J. Elfreth Watkins.[8] The popularity of *Jersey Genesis* kept the Leeds Devil / Jersey Devil folklore alive and possibly fueled a resurgence of sightings in the 1950s and 1960s.

While the Leeds Devil and Jersey Devil are synonymous when referring to the modern era monster, the Leeds Devil as it refers to the early settler Daniel Leeds is a different beast altogether, a monster born out of the intolerance men had for one another. Not as fun, but not a story that should be forgotten or lost. From now on whenever we mention the Leeds Devil, we're referring to pre-1909, while the Jersey Devil refers to the pop culture monster we know today.

Mothman and Humanoids

To most sky-monster fans, Mothman is a humanoid creature widely reported to have been seen in the Point Pleasant, West Virginia, area between November 1966 and December 1967. In his 1975 book *The Mothman Prophecies*, John Keel, ufologist, journalist, and Mothman investigator says no one knows who named the creature: "Some anonymous copy editor gave it a name, spun off from the Batman comic character who was then the subject of a popular TV series. He tagged the creature Mothman."[9]

Common Characteristics of Mothman Descriptions

- Six to seven feet tall
- Large, bat-like wings
- Large red eyes
- Very small head, if any
- Causes a feeling of doom
- Gets close to but never touches people

Some reports suggest Mothman is more the size of a large owl, also with big red eyes. Other witnesses have described legs that stretch out behind him in flight like those of a heron or crane. Some attach evil connotations to Mothman sightings and believe Mothman was present in Point Pleasant, West Virginia, one year prior to the Silver Bridge Collapse as a cause or premonition of that tragedy. Others attach good connotations or believe he offered a warning. Whatever the intent of this nighttime flier—and whatever people have witnessed—there is no way to prove or disprove what happened during that thirteen-month period. People will make up their minds based on the evidence we'll explore in this book.

What can't be disputed is that Mothman became a mainstay of pop-culture cryptids after the release of the 2002 movie *Mothman Prophecies,* starring Richard Gere and based on Keel's book. In real life, as explained in the book, Keel felt called to Point Pleasant to explore the sightings and better understand the phenomenon that had occurred in this small town along the Ohio River. Keel believed his presence was significant—that he needed to be in Point Pleasant. Together with locals, he explored sightings and tried to make sense of the creature's presence and why he felt a connection to it.

Behind the Mothman Story

Mothman came to into public consciousness after terrorizing two young couples cruising the back roads near an abandoned TNT plant. In the 1960s, Point Pleasant was situated amid long stretches of remote roadways with large tracts of unoccupied land between the Ohio River and rolling hills. Nights were dark and boring. The TNT plant had been an area of interest where teens met up to hang out and drag race. But on one particular night, even the TNT plant was deserted.

In an interview recorded in Donnie Sargent Jr. and Jeff Wamsley's *Mothman: The Facts Behind the Legend* (2016), nineteen-year-old Linda Scarberry (her married name at the time) states no one in the car had been drinking or using drugs. It was near midnight on a clear and cold night. She and her husband and friends were out "chasing parkers." When they came upon the old powerhouse building at the TNT plant, they saw a figure with large red eyes standing in the road.

"It had arms and legs like a muscular man." She further described it as being seven feet tall. "One of its wings [was] caught in a guide wire . . . and [it] was pulling and pulling on its wings with its hands. . . . Its hands were

really big." The two couples left the site but then returned to the location a little bit later. "[The creature] was sitting crouched down, with its arms around its legs and its wings tucked against its back."[10]

Within a year, over a thousand sightings throughout the Point Pleasant region were reported. When the Silver Bridge collapsed in December 1967, the sightings stopped. Interest in Mothman died out, or as some believe, he completed his task and disappeared.

Mothman Moves to Chicago and Other Humanoids

Witnesses filed over twenty reports of Mothman in Chicago between April and July 2017. An article in the July 29, 2017, edition of the *Chicago Tribune* states, "A woman walking her dog claimed she encountered a creature standing in the park. 'I saw a large man, probably seven feet or taller stand-

ing on the ground. It was solid black, but what really stood out were the large, and I do mean large, pair of wings that were folded behind him.'"[11]

Mothman might be the darling of some humanoids, but there are others that have been terrified by appearances across the country. In 1994, deep in the forests surrounding Mount Rainier, a young man was driving through the mountains when his pickup truck stalled. A large figure, at least nine feet tall, descended from the sky and landed in front of him. Covered in blueish fur, the creature had a wolf-like face and large wings. After what appeared to be a short rest, the creature flew away. To this day, travelers through this area sometimes glimpse the winged beast-man now known as Batsquatch.

In Houston in 1953, a twenty-three-year-old woman and two of her neighbors believe they may have seen an extraterrestrial, UFO, or supernatural entity when a seven-foot-tall, manlike figure landed in a tree near their home. He looked to be wearing a skintight suit and helmet. A soft glow surrounded his body. After the witnesses made a frightened police report, the *Houston Chronicle* followed up with a front-page story on what they dubbed "The Houston Batman." Years later, residents inside the city described a similar figure on a rooftop that appeared to be hiding.

> **FUN FACT:** While the Houston Batman has drifted into Houston history, he continues to be remembered nightly when crowds gather near the Waugh Drive Bridge to watch approximately 250,000 bats from a huge roost under the bridge wake up and fly into the night to feed.

Another famous humanoid story came out of Van Meter, Iowa, in 1908. The monster resembled a man with *Pteranodon* features that included a beak, a glowing horn, and a large wingspan. The creature appeared throughout the town, scaring residents as it alighted on lawns and the roofs of buildings. Several concerned citizens shot at the creature and then tracked it until it entered a mine shaft and apparently disappeared.

Are these entities all versions of the same creature? Perhaps exaggerations that resulted from nighttime encounters with oversized owls or bats? Could they be supernatural entities whose shape and form vary slightly but are made from the same demonic or angelic matter? Or were these apparitions manifestations of the Cold War atmosphere of paranoia and stories about UFOs and alien experimentation?

When discussing the paranormal or supernatural world, we must first understand our worldview and how our knowledge and belief systems drive our unique perceptions and interpretations of the phenomena. Doing this allows us to stand firm in our own beliefs while tolerating the diverse beliefs of others.

2

WHO'S WHO IN THE AMERICAN SKY?

Introduction to the Thunderbirds and *Pteranodons*

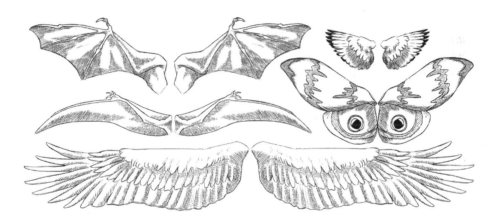

THE SKIES ARE FULL OF WONDEROUS CREATURES—LARGE, SMALL, colorful, and plain. They exist in a space humans cannot reach. We observe from the ground, unable to close the distance. Whether our observations are influenced by our religious beliefs, our imaginations, or simply by what we witness, the world of flying cryptids is intriguing to us all.

We've attempted to capture a wide variety of cryptids and legendary flying creatures to inform and entertain our readers. This is not a comprehensive list, nor is it necessarily a credible list. We've accessed multiple resources and presented the most common information available about flying cryptids and creatures that have existed throughout history, either in legend or reality.

ACHIYALABOPA

Wingspan Incredibly large.

Physical Description Rainbow-colored feathers; feathers sharp as knives.

Demeanor Can be authoritarian and strike disrespectful humans but prefers to rule with kindness.

Supernatural Powers Legendary, god-like figure, god of the sky.

Location Arizona and New Mexico, Pueblo and other Native American legends.

Notes Achiyalabopa may be another name for Thunderbird, but they differ in temperament. Where Thunderbird is aggressive like a thunderstorm, Achiyalabopa is calm and beautiful like a rainbow.

THE AWFUL

Wingspan Twenty feet.

Physical Description Similar to a griffin, with grey wings, a long serpentine tail, and talon-like claws.

Demeanor Threatening.

Location Richford and Berkshire, Vermont.

Notes Legend states that in 1900, two sawmill workers first saw the creature as they crossed Main Street Bridge near the Canadian border. The beast glared down at them from the nearby Boright Building. While it's hurt no one, the creature's menacing features frighten many who have reported seeing it.

In 1925, horror writer H. P. Lovecraft had been staying with friends in southern Vermont when he heard news of the terrifying creature. He traveled to Richford and spoke with eyewitnesses before returning home to Rhode Island. He later revealed that the Awful inspired many of his terrifying creatures.

AVERASBORO GALLINIPPER

Wingspan Size of a large hawk; three-to-five-foot wingspan.

Physical Description Giant mosquito.

Demeanor Vicious.

Supernatural Powers Can pierce a man with ease using its stinger and drain his blood in a single gulp.

Location Averasboro, North Carolina.

Notes In the 1850s, Irish immigrants to the Cape Fear region reported the presence of giant mosquitoes. Lumbermen who worked the swamps of North Carolina also feared a creature called the Gallinipper. While the Gallinipper is thought to be a fearsome supernatural critter, there is also a large species of mosquito native to the southeastern United States called the American Gallinipper.

An Iroquoian legend of the Tuscarora claimed that North Carolina is the birthplace of the mosquito. It is said that in the beginning there was only one mosquito, named *Ro-Tay-Yo*. This beast terrorized the people, and he was eventually killed. When the arrow pierced his heart, thousands of little mosquitos dispersed from it. That is why we have so many tiny mosquitos today.

BATSQUATCH

Wingspan As wide as a road (eight to ten feet).

Physical Description Nine-foot-tall flying primate with yellow eyes, wolf-like muzzle, bluish fur, sharp teeth, bird-like feet, and leathery bat wings.

Demeanor Sinister; considered a bad omen.

Supernatural Powers Has the ability to manipulate car engines or electronics.

Location Near Mount St. Helens, Washington.

Notes Eyewitnesses around the Mount St. Helens area began seeing Batsquatch after the volcano erupted in 1980. In one account, an eyewitness reported the creature landed in front of his truck after the engine died. The bat-winged, hairy figure stared, then flew off.

A similar creature was reported in Texas in the mid-1970s. Two brothers were driving down a long stretch of road when a bat-winged humanoid dropped down in front of them. Not far away, a father and son claimed they were attacked while hunting deer. The bat-winged beast swooped down and grabbed the father, attempting to carry him off. The son shot at the creature and freed the father, who suffered broken ribs and talon marks.

In pop culture, Batsquatch has inspired a craft beer manufactured by Rogue. On their website, they state, "What better way to honor the elusive legend than with a hazy IPA? Perfect for camping and potentially making a new friend. This juicy, cloudy IPA features intense tropical flavors and aromas."

BIG BIRD

Wingspan Twelve feet.

Physical Description Large and black with red markings on its back. Five feet tall with featherless, bat-like wings; bald head with a monkey-like face and red eyes; long talons.

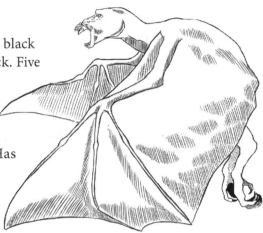

Demeanor Can be aggressive. Has attempted to attack and carry off victims.

Location Brownsville, Texas, and throughout the Rio Grande Valley.

Encounter Date Early January 1976. Sporadically thereafter.

Notes On New Year's Day, two girls were playing in their backyard when they noticed a large animal standing near a canal about one hundred yards away. The girls ran into the house and found a pair of binoculars. They could see the giant bird-like creature watching them. It let out a loud, high-pitched screech before it took off. The next day, one of the girls' fathers found a twelve-by-eight inch, three-toed track behind their house and called the local TV station.

A couple of days later, two police officers saw a large bird swoop over their patrol cars. More disturbing was an account on January 7, when a loud thump sounded against the side of a family's home. The man of the house grabbed a knife and went outside to see what caused the noise. On the ground lay a giant creature with wings, but it didn't exactly look like a bird. The creature rose and made a pulsing noise in its throat. They stared at one another; then the bird backed away.

Throughout this time, area ranches experienced cow mutilations. One man reported a near abduction by a giant bird, who swooped down and tried to grab ahold of him. Area newspapers ran more and more stories as others came forward to talk about their sightings. The news traveled across the country, causing a frenzy that brought tourists and news reporters to the area in hopes of catching a glimpse. By the end of January, the excitement had died down, but sightings have continued to take place across southern Texas to this day.[1]

FUN FACT: Big Bird is allegedly protected by the state for fear that a hunter will mistake a rare or endangered bird for the cryptid.

CRAWFORDSVILLE MONSTER

Wingspan Twenty feet long and eight feet wide.
Physical Description Rectangular shaped body, resembling an eel; several fins run down its side; eye in the mouth and three jaws.
Location Crawfordsville, Indiana.

Notes In 1891, two ice delivery men and a minister and his wife saw the creature fly through the air, making a wheezing sound. "It flapped like a flag in the winds . . . and squirmed as though suffering."[2] The Crawfordsville monster is an "atmospheric beast," which means it could be an otherworldly creature.

CUMBERLAND DRAGON

Wingspan Unknown. The account states the creature jumped high into the air, but there is no mention of wings.

Physical Description Bipedal, with its two feet leaving footprints like those of a goose. Brownish-black scales with light-yellow spots, a white tuft of fur around its head, red eyes.

Demeanor Native Americans in the area believed the creature would kill a man with its breath if he did not immerse himself in water.

Location Cumberland Mountains, Tennessee.

Notes Only reported to have been sighted once near the Cumberland Mountains. This account was recorded in the *Caledonian Mercury* on December 4, 1794, and mentioned that Ensign McDonald and a partner saw the unusual creature while on a spy mission.

DEMON LEAPER

Physical Description Gargoyle or bat-like, with leathery skin and long talons.

Demeanor Frightening but playful, some witnesses report he would fly down and poke people but hurt no one.

Supernatural Powers Can leap and fly long distances.

Location Louisville, Kentucky.

Note Most often seen atop a local Baptist church, but the creature would also fly to the roofs of other buildings and hop along their edges. A September 12, 1880, article in the *New York Times* talked about the Demon Leaper and reported on a similar creature sighted on Coney Island.[3]

Flatwoods Monster

Wingspan No wings, but it hovers or floats. Ten feet tall and four feet wide.

Physical Description Robotic suit / spacecraft; wears a cowl in the shape of the ace of spades; round red head, glowing green / orange eyes; body looks as if it was made of metallic armor.

Demeanor With claw-like hands, it moves with a direct approach through a burning mist. Eyewitnesses felt threatened and ran from the scene.

Supernatural Powers Floats and emits a glow.

Location Flatwoods, West Virginia.

Notes On September 12, 1952, three boys saw a ball of fire fall from the sky and land atop a hill in Braxton County. Along with their parents and a few other boys, they went to investigate. A local paper reported, "Seven Braxton County residents on Saturday reported seeing a ten-foot Frankenstein-like monster in the hills above Flatwoods." At first they saw what appeared to be a pair of bright eyes in a tree. Then, walking out of a dense mist, came a creature with a blood-red body and a glowing green face.

The next morning, a reporter found prints and a black goo. The story was picked up by national radio and big papers all over the country, leading to an investigation by the U.S. Air Force's Project Blue Book. Also known as the Braxton County Monster, the Phantom of Flatwoods, or the Green Monster.

In pop culture, the Flatwoods Monster appears in games such as *NES*, *Amagon*, *Space Harrier II*, and *The Legend of Zelda Majora's Mask*, among several others.

Flying Manta Rays

Wingspan Approximately twenty-five feet; bigger than a car and wider than a two-lane road.

Physical Description Grayish-black, translucent, smooth-winged shape like that of a manta ray.

Demeanor Unknown.

Supernatural Powers May be able to disappear or blend in with its surroundings.

Location West Virginia, near water.

Note This creature is considered an atmospheric beast. In 2004, a couple driving near the Ohio River in West Virginia saw movement in the sky. A translucent creature that looked like a giant manta ray swooped down over their car and then disappeared out of sight. In another part of West Virginia, a mother and daughter reported seeing a similar creature.

Frank Shaw's Gargoyle, aka the Houston Bat Man

Due to variability in witness accounts and terminology, some believe these to be different humanoid creatures.

Wingspan Unknown, but very large.

Physical Description Dark in color but surrounded by a soft glow of light; resembles a gargoyle; humanoid with a large cape draped over its shoulders. Cape could also be draping wrinkly skin or bat-like wings.

Demeanor Malevolent aura, monstrous. On other occasions, passive and observant.

Supernatural Powers Flying. Some accounts report materializing and dematerializing.

Location South Texas, predominately the Houston area.

Notes The first sighting took place in the historic Houston Heights neighborhood, northwest of downtown Houston, when a young woman and her neighbors saw a humanoid creature land in a tree near the house. The creature watched them for several seconds and then shot into the sky, leaving a glowing trail.

　　Frank Shaw, a NASA archivist at Houston's Johnson Space Center, also claimed to have had a terrifying run-in with the Houston Batman or a creature similar to it. As he was leaving the Space Center, he glanced up and saw a black, gargoyle-like figure perched on the edge of one of the buildings. After reporting this event to his supervisor, Shaw learned he wasn't alone. In addition to two other sightings of the creature, two of the base's German shepherds had been mauled and an investigation was already underway. Shaw's daughter reported that he was later visited by Men in Black who warned him not to talk about what he witnessed.

Iowa Dragons

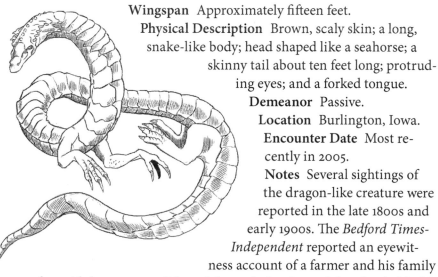

Wingspan Approximately fifteen feet.
Physical Description Brown, scaly skin; a long, snake-like body; head shaped like a seahorse; a skinny tail about ten feet long; protruding eyes; and a forked tongue.
Demeanor Passive.
Location Burlington, Iowa.
Encounter Date Most recently in 2005.
Notes Several sightings of the dragon-like creature were reported in the late 1800s and early 1900s. The *Bedford Times-Independent* reported an eyewitness account of a farmer and his family who said the creature slithered through the sky and then landed in his field. After a short time, it flew off. In 2005, a man and woman encountered the creature while driving.

Jersey Devil

Wingspan Four to five feet.
Physical Description Three to four feet tall. Head of a horse; body of a kangaroo; bat wings; serpentine or forked tail; feet of a goat. Some accounts say it has the head of a ram and the face of a monkey. On the ground or rooftops it hops like a bird. Emits a high, piercing scream.
Demeanor Eats livestock, flies at people. Said to be pure evil.
Supernatural Powers Some people believe the Jersey Devil is responsible for the bad things that happen in and around the Pine Barrens and that it has the ability to harm people without them knowing it.
Location Pine Barrens, New Jersey.
Notes America's oldest original monster/cryptid. Much more about this cryptid in chapter 3, "History and Legends."

KANSAS CITY WINGED DEMON

Wingspan Twelve to eighteen feet.

Physical Description Black in color; about the size of a man with a humanlike face; leathery, bat-like wings; covered in hair; has a beak and red eyes.

Demeanor Menacing, as it has been known to shake a house or run into the side of a house.

Supernatural Powers None noted.

Location Kansas City, Missouri.

Notes Some speculate this might be a type of pterosaur, as it wobbles when it walks. Seen four to five times.

One sighting, which occurred in 2005, tells of two women and a man who witnessed a giant bird "hopping awkwardly from branch to branch . . . as if attempting to become airborne."[4] When it landed on the ground, the group ran indoors. A loud thud sounded against the side of the house, then the demon bird disappeared. Six years later, it returned and was seen by others, leaving a trail of terrified yet curious witnesses.

LONE PINE MOUNTAIN DEVIL

Wingspan Unknown.

Physical Description Multiple large, furry wings (two sets), talons, venomous fangs.

Demeanor Fierce and deadly. Will attack humans.

Supernatural Powers Some believe the creature attacks or hunts people who disrespect nature and wildlife but also those who doubt its existence or disturb its habitat.

Location Sierra Nevada; more recent sightings near Alabama Hills, California.

Note Forty-niners expanded the legend of this creature as a way to explain groups of dead they wandered upon whose insides had been eaten away. For more details about this creature, please see chapter 5, "Fact or Fiction?"

LOUISIANA THUNDERBIRD

Wingspan Unknown but large.

Physical Description Black and grayish with feathers; approximately eight feet tall.

Demeanor Aggressive toward animals.

Supernatural Powers None noted.

Location Marthaville, Lousiana.

Notes In the spring of 1978, a group of kids tromped through the woods to a cow pasture. There they saw an extremely large bird walking toward them. Frightened, they ran back to the house. Cow mutilations had been reported in the area.

More recently, in Slidell, Louisiana, a woman saw a giant bird flying overhead. She said it had no feathers, teeth in its beak, and what looked like long hair covering its body.

MOTHMAN

Wingspan Ten to fifteen feet.

Physical Description Seven-foot-tall bipedal, winged humanoid; black, grey, or brownish fur or feathers; red eyes; not always reported to have a neck.

Demeanor Passive, but leaves an unsettling feeling of doom.

Supernatural Powers Precognitive; some believe his presence is to communicate a future tragedy so it can be prevented. Others believe the creature is an omen. Able to fly over 100 miles per hour.

Locations Point Pleasant, West Virginia; Ashland and Elizabethtown, Kentucky; Chicago, Illinois.

Notes In September of 1978, miners in Freiburg, Germany, reported a dark, humanoid figure with wings blocking the entrance to their mine. It let out a scream, frightening the men. Soon after, a loud explosion sounded as the mine collapsed. This creature became known as the Freiburg Shrieker.

Survivors of the 1986 Chernobyl nuclear disaster in Ukraine also claimed to have seen a mothman figure flying through the smoke and ruins of the explosion.

NAPA REBOBS

Wingspan The wings appear bat-like and not overly large, but no official size has been recorded.

Physical Description Part monkey, part robot. Some stories suggest a monkey-human or monkey-bat combo.

Demeanor Aggressive and will attack children.

Location Napa Valley, California.

Notes Legend states a mad scientist attempted to combine monkeys and robots. If you wait at the end of Patrick Road—named after the original landowners—until dark, the rebobs will fly out of the trees. But beware—they've been known to climb through windows and abduct children.

At the end of Patrick Road is a military building, which has prompted some conspiracists to believe a "mad scientist" conducted secret experiments there, either to create a new weapon or provide a smokescreen to detract attention away from the real purpose of the facility.

PIASA BIRD

Wingspan Very large.

Physical Description The mural on the cliffside that people call the Piasa Bird depicts a body shaped like a horse, with long fangs that rise out of the lower jaw, deerlike antlers, stubby legs with talons on the feet, long spiked tail, and very large wings. In the Piasa monster story, the bird is more birdlike, with the body and talons of a massive raptor.

Demeanor Sneaky and vicious.

Supernatural Powers Very fast and skilled at hunting. Powerful enough to carry off a full-grown man.

Location Near Alton, Illinois, along the Mississippi River.

Notes The legend of the Piasa Bird states that Native Americans painted the Piasa Bird on the face of a bluff to honor the great spirit for saving their tribe, but this is a fictional account. Please read the complete story in chapter 5, "Fact or Fiction?"

SNALLYGASTER

Wingspan Twenty-five to thirty feet.

Physical Description Half reptile, half bird; has a long, metallic beak with a tentacle-like tongue and sharp teeth; talons of steel.

Demeanor Fearsome. The creature swoops out of the sky, snatching animals and sometimes children off the ground. Some claim this creature sucks the blood of its victims.

Location Maryland and Virginia.

Notes The name Snallygaster is derived from the German *Schneller Geist* which means "quick spirit." Legend holds that when Germans emigrated to America, they brought the creature with them. To keep it away, people painted seven-pointed stars on their barns.

In 1909, George C. Rhoderick, editor of the *Middletown Valley Register*, perpetrated a hoax, claiming several local residents encountered a beast with "enormous wings; a long, pointed bill; claws like steel hooks; and an eye in the center of its forehead." Riding on the heels of recent Jersey Devil publicity, Rhoderick hoped to drum up business for his newspaper.

In pop culture, the Snallygaster appears in the 2018 Bethesda game *Fallout 76*, the same year the Dragon Distillery of Frederick, Maryland, released a blended whiskey named Snallygaster.

SOUTH CAROLINA THUNDERBIRD

Wingspan Twelve to fifteen feet.

Physical Description White or orange eyes, no feathers, leathery wings, crest behind the head, long tail.

Demeanor Aggressively approaches vehicles.

Location Throughout South Carolina.

Notes In 2004, a couple driving through the woods near Myrtle Beach heard a loud flapping noise. Looking up, they saw what looked like a whitish *Pteranodon*. Since then, more sightings have occurred throughout the state.

Native American lore of the Santee, a Siouan-speaking tribe, calls these creatures *Wakinyan*, which means "flying thunderer." Siouan-speaking tribes are traditionally from the Great Plains where some Thunderbird stories refer to a *Pteranodon*-type flying creature (likely because they saw *Pteranodon* fossil remains throughout the chalk beds in the area). Perhaps this lore stayed with the Santee as they migrated eastward.

VAN METER MONSTER

Wingspan Eight feet

Physical Description Humanoid creature with membranous, bat-like wings; a unicorn-like horn that glows; and three-toed prints. Leaves a horrendous smell in its wake.

Demeanor Looks menacing but would rather retreat than fight.

Supernatural Powers Is able to project a blinding light out of its forehead.

Location Van Meter, Iowa.

Notes Seen by several prominent men in 1903 before it retreated to a mine and disappeared.

3

HISTORY AND LEGENDS

In the Beginning

In pre-Columbian North America, indigenous people were mobile and often migrated to follow food sources, carrying with them the customs, teachings, and oral traditions of the previous generation. Their dependence on the land and interaction with the environment allowed them to become experts on nature, including plants, animals, and fossils. Interpretations of what they encountered in nature were closely connected with their spiritual beliefs.

According to one legend, long ago the people from the Sioux and Assiniboine (tribes of the Great Plains) went camping near a big lake. In the middle of the lake there was an island, and there a battle between a Thunderbird and a water monster took place. As the Thunderbird picked the monster up off the island, electricity floated through the air and sparked many forest fires. A devastating blizzard followed. Then the lake dried up. Many years later, descendants of the storyteller returned to this dried-up location and found a turtle skeleton as big as a man, and the remains of several horned animals.

This story may have been a way to explain the menagerie of fossils found lying together in the dry lakebeds of Kansas. It may also incorporate the Shawnee origins legend that they were brought to this world on the shell of a turtle. According to Iroquois scholar Barbara Mann, "bones and parts of animals, including fossils, were considered powerful 'earth medicine.' Hunting parties would go on long treks to collect the large bones of game animals to be used in their hunting medicine. Fossils and ancient bones were not foreign to the indigenous people of North America."[1]

Many scientists believe one of the oldest flying birds on record is *Archaeopteryx*, whose fossilized skeleton was found in the mid- to late 1800s in southern Germany. In the last decade, scientists have identified another kind of winged creature in China and named it *Xiaotingia zhengi*. The fossil shows faint feather markings and is believed to be older than *Archaeopteryx*, but some debate whether these creatures have more in common with reptiles than birds. While no one can pinpoint the exact age or habits of either creature, we can be certain they existed. Both fossilized skeletons offer a nice depiction of what ancient flying creatures looked like. Yet neither species were of the massive size of the Thunderbirds mentioned in many Native American legends.

Some paleontologists and historians have suggested stories of Thunderbirds may have been based on discoveries of *Pteranodon* (commonly known as a pterodactyl) in the American Great Plains. The first *Pteranodon* fossil found by European settlers was discovered in Kansas in 1876. The Kansas-Nebraska chalk beds showed several marine creatures and flying reptiles preserved together. Findings of water and sky creatures buried together in the chalk beds may explain why several Thunderbird legends tell of the sky spirit overpowering the water monster. Perhaps the fossils most likely to be associated with Thunderbird are the remains of giant birds called teratorns. With a wingspan between twelve to seventeen feet, these giant birds existed throughout the American Southwest, and in her book *Fossil Legends of the First Americans* Adrienne Mayor notes that teratorn fossils "almost always exist with human occupation sites."[2]

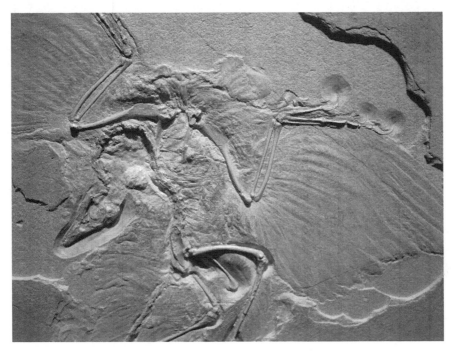

Cast of an *Archaeopteryx lithographica* fossil that currently resides in the Australian Museum, Sydney. Photo by Denise Chan is licensed under CC by SA 2.0.

Symbolic Meaning of the Thunderbird

The symbolic meanings associated with the Thunderbird in Native American legend vary from one tribal region to another, but most tend to fall into one or more of the categories listed below. (The regional sections following this introduction will offer more specific details.)

1. Figure of Authority: The Thunderbird is thought to pass judgment. It is a powerful force that can strike down bad men as well as those who wander too close to its home. Only the most powerful and successful chiefs and families use the Thunderbird in their crest. The Thunderbird should be respected by all because he brings life and death.

2. Symbol of Sustenance: When the Thunderbird flaps its heavy wings, waves of thunder vibrate through the air, warning man of incoming storms. Lightning shoots from its eyes, deadly yet nourishing, bringing rains to water the land.

   Researchers speculate these large birds were associated with storms because, like the eagle, they followed air drafts to stay in flight and may have migrated with the seasons. It is reported that long ago some Native people appealed to the Thunderbird for help during times of famine. It is said the Thunderbird helped, but in return wished to be placed at the top of a totem pole with its wings stretched out.

3. Omen of War: Legend tells that when the thunder rumbles, it is a sign the spirits in the sky are at war. This is the cry of the Thunderbird. Western tribes constructed war huts as their ceremonial processions began. These huts were made from cedar—the sacred tree of the Thunderbird. In the East, Iroquois and Shawnee performed war dances with exact precision to honor the Thunderbird and ensure a victory.

4. Divine Presence: Many northwestern tribes believe the cedar forests are a spiritual place where the Thunderbird dwells. They are also places no one should enter because this is where the Thunderbird rules the activity of the skies. Other tribes believe Thunderbird dwells above the clouds.

The Haida of the Northwest created elaborate masks in the image of Thunderbird. People wore these masks during rituals, sometimes allowing the beaks to open and reveal the face of the human. This symbolized the transformation of a human into the form of a Thunderbird. Haida belief states the Thunderbird visited great hunters and elders on their deathbed. The bird would fly the human's soul into the cedar forests where they would forever reside.

Northwest Coast Indians devised mechanical masks with movable parts to reveal the human face, illustrating their belief that the human spirit could take animal form and vice versa.

5. Prophesying Messenger: Hearing the Thunderbird flap its wings to signify war was also believed to foretell victory, especially when song and dance rituals were followed.

Thunderbirds and *Pteranodons* by Region

Pacific Northwest

The vast red cedar forests of the Pacific Northwest, where eagles hunt for salmon and condors were once common, are home to several of the earliest Thunderbird stories. Also known as the Rain Bird, some believed this life-bringer also passed judgment and carried out punishments. Listed below are a few tribes who recognize the Thunderbird in their spirituality. Stories vary according to traditional beliefs. In some the majestic godlike bird is praised and in others feared, but in all cases there is respect for this iconic creature.

The Chinook, or "canoe people," lived north of the Columbia River near its mouth, while their relatives, the Clatsop, resided on the south bank. Both tribes relied heavily on salmon and other resources from in and around the river. They used the wood from the tall red cedars to construct plank houses and pieces of their clothing, and they were superb canoe builders. They buried their dead in canoes, believing the boat would carry the body and personal effects into the afterlife. They also believed a great spirit was entwined with a mythology that described protective animal spirits.

The Chinook lived in plank houses called Big Houses and slept on elevated structures covered with reed mats. The houses ranged from twenty to sixty feet wide and from fifty to one hundred and fifty feet long. The interior consisted of a central communal space surrounded by sleeping and storage areas partitioned off with wooden dividers or animal skins. Each home featured a portal or entryway totem pole that identified the owner and family of the house. As many as fifty extended relatives might live in one structure.

Controlling the northern mouth of the Columbia River, the Chinook were used to seeing European goods and white traders. On October 26, 1805, two Chinook chiefs and several men welcomed the Corps of Discovery—otherwise known as the Lewis and Clark expedition. They exchanged gifts and spent time together as other Chinook villagers came to see the explorers and offer gifts. Tension ensued when a Chinook slave stole from the expedition. After retrieving their goods, however, the Corps left the territory without an ounce of bloodshed.

According to Chinook legend, long ago, Thunderbird, who was part human and part spirit, laid five eggs on top of Saddle Mountain in Oregon. An ogress rolled the Thunderbird eggs down the mountain and five men, each of a different color, were "born" as creatures of the sky because that is where the Thunderbird lives. These men searched the valley and found women growing out of the earth in various stages of development. It is said the Chinook chief plucked his wife from a rock. Her arms left holes in this rock as if she had been hugging it. This is the origin story for the Chinook

Tribe. As they grew in number, they split up and moved down the Columbia River.

THE KWAKIUTL

At one time, Kwakiutl was a name given to all the Kwakwaka'wakw—people who spoke the language Kwakwala—who lived in the Pacific Northwest. Today, the name refers to just one tribe living at Fort Rupert, but at the time of European contact in 1786, the Kwakwaka'wakw comprised some twenty tribes or family groups, each having its own chief. The tribes were nomads, who moved from winter clamming beds to spring smelt runs up the rivers, to summer fishing grounds. Two or more tribes often shared the same village site, living in plank houses. Group boundaries constantly shifted, causing splits, mergers, and conflicts.

Despite their mobility and differences, all of these groups believed Thunderbird was a divine protector. The Kwakiutl also believe Tsonaqua, or "Wild Woman of the Woods," is a form of Bigfoot. Not fully human, she is a fearsome giant of the forest who steals children and eats them. However, special types of encounters with her can lead to wealth and supernatural powers. There is a story about a chief named Splashing-Waters who was being tormented by Tsonaqua. Kwun-kwane-kulegui, also known as Thunderbird, turned Tsonaqua into stone. From then on Chief Splashing-Waters revered Thunderbird and called him the Protector of Man. On totem poles, the Kwakiutl people placed the Wild Woman of the Woods beneath the Thunderbird to show all that the powerful bird would always rule over her. At festivals, they honor Thunderbird by the wearing of masks during songs and dances.

THE TOTEM POLE

While the Chinook and the Kwakiutl adopted the tradition of carving totem poles, it first began with the Haida, Tlingit, and Tsimshian—First Nations who lived along the Pacific coast in British Columbia, Alaska, and Washington. The totem pole was a precise art form with carvings that showed lineage, family legends, social status, inheritance, power, and privilege. Often serving a similar role to a family crest, the pole was erected in front of the home or over the entranceway and passed down through generations.

Native Americans carved totem poles out of cedar—sacred to the Thunderbird—in the shape of animals that symbolized guardian spirits and mythological creatures. Totem poles usually celebrated a great accomplishment of a living or deceased family member. The figures were arranged from top to bottom, but the sequence of the carvings beneath the Thunderbird (if present) were not a sign of their importance.

During a time before the written word, people would also carve their personal stories onto a totem pole. One such story, shared by Anne Siberell in her children's book *Whale in the Sky*, tells how Thunderbird watched over all the animals on the land and in the sea. According to Siberell, as Thunderbird was flying over the water, Raven approached and told him Whale was chasing the salmon. Thunderbird quickly flew off and found Whale just before he entered the river, which would have disturbed the homes of the frogs and fish. He picked up the whale in his talons. Whale struggled to get away, but Thunderbird flew higher and higher. Finally, he dropped him onto a mountain. All the creatures living in the river were safe. Whale grew weak on the mountain. He promised to stay out of the river if Thunderbird allowed him to return to the sea. Thunderbird

Totem pole with Thunderbird. ©Tomacco. Shutterstock Image.

clapped his wings causing a thunderous vibration. Whale slid down the mountain and back into the water.[3]

Coastal Native Americans and First People generally viewed whales as compassionate, solitary creatures. They associated them with wisdom and awareness of the spiritual realm. But several legends and stories tell of an ongoing battle between Whale and Thunderbird, both of supernatural power and size. While there is often no clear victor, the stories sometimes offer an explanation for the damage caused by natural disasters.

Another legend of Thunderbird tells of a great flood that covered a significant portion of the earth. During this flood, Thunderbird fought Mimlos-Whale in a long and brutal battle. The Thunderbird grabbed Mimlos-

Whale with his mighty talons and dragged him to his mountain nest. But the whale was smart, escaped the nest, and found refuge in the water again. Every time Thunderbird captured Mimlos-Whale, there would be a great fight that was so loud it shook the mountains and uprooted the trees. This battle went on for a long time until finally Thunderbird grew tired. He allowed Mimlos-Whale to escape into the depths of the ocean. This is why the killer whale can still be found in the ocean today. The treeless prairies found on the Olympic Peninsula are said to have resulted from these battles between Thunderbird and Mimlos-Whale.

THE CASCADE RAPIDS

Prior to 1896, river navigation of the Cascade Rapids on the Columbia River presented many challenges and great danger to Americans traveling west.

The first European Americans from the east to encounter them were Lewis and Clark and the Corps of Discovery. Regarding the rapids, William Clark wrote in his journal on October 31, 1805:

> This Great Shute or falls is about ½ a mile with the water of this great river Compressed within the Space of 150 paces in which there is great numbers of both large and Small rocks, water passing with great velocity forming & boiling in a most horriable manner, with a fall of about 20 feet, below it widens to about 200 paces and current gentle for a Short distance. a Short distance above is three Small rockey Islands, and at the head of those falls, three Small rockey Islands are Situated Crosswise the river, Several rocks above in the river & 4 large rocks in the head of the Shute; those obstructions together with the high Stones which are continually brakeing loose from the mountain on the Stard Side and roleing down into the Shute aded to those which brake loose from those Islands above and lodge in the Shute, must be the Cause of the rivers daming up.[4]

Those pushing along the Oregon Trail eventually came to the edge of the Columbia River at what French fur trappers called the dalles—a word meaning gorge or gutter—because the river cut a narrow passage of dangerous rapids through the Cascade Range. For nearly three years, this was the end of the land trail. Settlers had to purchase or rent rafts and accompany their wagons on the rough waters (unless they walked with the cattle). Many lost their lives.

In 1845, Philip Foster and Sam Barlow built the Barlow (toll) Road to detour around the rapids, but due to cost and the comparable dangers, some pioneers still chose the rapids. Steamboats could not go upriver, but skilled captains could bring them down. To aid in the passage, the Cascade Canal and Locks was built around the rapids in 1896. This worked to facilitate travel, but to respond to the rising demand for flood control and hydroelectricity, one of the most innovative American industrial projects of the twentieth century was planned. The construction of the Bonneville Lock and Dam began in 1934, and the facility opened for operation in 1937. Today, it continues to be an important energy resource and the largest provider of electricity in the Pacific Northwest.

During construction of the Bonneville Lock and Dam, the older Cascade locks and rapids were submerged beneath the Bonneville Reservoir, also known as Bonneville Lake. They named this landmark for Benjamin Bonneville, an Army Colonel who served in the Mexican-American and Civil Wars. He explored the western territories while working as a fur trader and was made famous by the writings of Washington Irving in a book called *The Adventures of Captain Bonneville* (1837). As Bonneville explored territories in the Pacific Northwest in 1832, he drew one of the first maps of the interior west, helping chart what would become the Oregon Trail.

But was there a time when no dam, no waterfall, and no rapids existed? No one knows for sure, but the following story offers an explanation of how the Cascade Rapids possibly came to be. We find this story on various sites across the internet, but its origin appears to be unknown. It could be a modern tale or a remnant of folklore that has survived across the years. Regardless, the tale offers another interesting story about Thunderbird.

THE BRIDGE OF THE GODS

There was a time when the animal people feared Thunderbird. The great bird lived near the setting sun and had created five mountains, threatening to kill any of the animal people who tried to pass over them. The wolf people did not believe him, and they sent five people to cross the mountain range. Together, they stepped on one of the mountains and immediately fell down dead.

Next, five brothers from the grizzly bear clan went. In the same way, they stepped on the mountain and instantly died.

"We will go," announced one of the cougar people. "We will leap over the mountains." He and his four brothers set out. They leapt and died in unison.

Now, it was the beavers' turn. Five brothers tried to drill under the mountain but died as soon as they started.

The coyote people could talk to the mountains. Coyote's five sons left home to speak with the mountains, hoping they could convince them to move. When they had not returned after five nights, father coyote was sure they had died. He cried out mournfully and prayed to the spirit chief for help. After he cried and prayed for a long time, Coyote heard a voice.

The spirit chief told him that because Thunderbird had made the law, it could not be broken, but there was something Coyote could do. The spirit chief told him to travel to the Above-World, collect a small feather from Eagle's youngest son, and then fast for ten days and ten nights. He said the smallest eagle feathers have power because they grow near the heart. This power would allow Coyote to defeat Thunderbird.

Coyote did as he was told. Eagle agreed to help because the command came from the spirit chief. Coyote fasted for ten days and ten nights, and then he was turned into a feather like the one Eagle had given him. He floated through the air toward the five mountains and the distant sun where Thunderbird lived. Still a good distance away, Coyote made a low rumbling noise.

Thunderbird heard the noise and feared he was in danger. He was the only one allowed to make such a rumbling sound. Three times, Coyote directed the sound toward the sun. Then he moved closer and projected an even louder rumble. Thunderbird grew angry and threatened to kill whoever was making the noise. He roared loudly, sending the tiny feather that was Coyote high into the air.

Thunderbird could not see him and was afraid. He knew if another wave of sound came, he would die. He dove deep into the great river, trying to hide from the powerful spirit threatening to kill him.

Coyote prayed to the spirit chief one more time. "Help me kill Thunderbird so my people and my sons will live." The spirit chief heard Coyote and helped him. As Thunderbird sank deeper into the water, Coyote let out the loudest rumble of all. The entire earth shook. The five mountains crumbled and fell.

Pieces of the mountain, floating down the Great River, formed islands along its course. Thunderbird died, and his giant body formed a great bridge above the river. The five sons of Coyote and all the other animal people who had been killed by Thunderbird came back to life.

Hundreds of years passed, but the great bridge (formed from the rocks that had been Thunderbird's body) still stood above the river. It was there long after the first Indians came to the earth. The Indians always called it the "Bridge of the Gods."

The Great Plains

From the base of the Rocky Mountains, the Great Plains stretch three hundred to seven hundred miles to the east and roughly three thousand miles from Texas to the northern border of Canada. Two types of Native Americans have lived in this region: those who farmed and lived sedentary lives along the rivers and those who became nomads. The latter grew in number as they acquired horses and began chasing the buffalo. They traveled across the sweeping plains and continued the tradition of using stories to explain natural phenomenon.

THE LAKOTA SIOUX

In the Black Hills of South Dakota, the Lakota Sioux ceremonial season began with the "Return of the Thunder Beings." They believed their return marked the beginning of spring, a time when the flowers and plants started to bloom, the buffalo and other migrating birds and animals returned to the area, and animals in hibernation awakened. The ceremonies were a celebration of life.

But the Thunder Beings also brought destructive storms to the land. They were respected because they had the power both to give life and take it away. They could destroy with the wind, bring flood or drought, or set the plains on fire with lightning. At the same time, they awakened and renewed the land by bringing rains that sustained all earthly life.

The Lakota believed Wakinyan, meaning Thunderbird, was one of the first creatures that existed. As one of the Thunder Beings, he could take a spiritual or animal form. Lakota legend described Thunder Beings as birdlike. Their wings produced the sound of thunder, and lightning shot from their eyes.

Insects and reptiles were also considered first creations. Unktehi, the evil water monster, ruled over them. When Unktehi grew large and became violent, Thunderbird petrified him with lightning, forcing the creature deep into the rocks.

Is it possible the Native Americans observed the bones of large fish and fishlike creatures embedded in rock, similar to what we can see now today in fossil beds? If there is an element of truth to the following legend, then the Lakota Sioux may also have observed large fossilized birds alongside ancient marine creatures.

> Long, long ago, before the white man came to America, a party of Sioux Indian warriors went out hunting. They had left their village far behind. Before they realized it, the group of braves found themselves alone in the bare and rocky badlands of the West.
>
> Suddenly the sky darkened. The broken hills took on a strange color under the stormy clouds. As the braves huddled together, feeling tiny in that empty land, a blazing zigzag of lightning ripped the sky. There was a clap of thunder that shook the earth.
>
> Looking up in terror, the Indians thought they saw the shape of a giant bird falling to earth. Less courageous men would have hurried home to their faraway village, thankful for their safety. But these were Sioux Indian braves, and they lived up to their proud name. They went off to find that bird.
>
> The band of hunters traveled over the badlands for days until they came at last to the spot where they thought the giant bird had fallen. Nothing was

left of the terrible creature except its bones, and nearby in some loose rocks, a scattering of thunderstones.

The Indians shuddered as they looked at the monster's skeleton. The bird had fallen so hard that its bones partly sank into the rock. But the braves could see that its wingspread was as long as four tall men standing on top of one another. The strange creature had fierce claws on its wings and on its feet. The beak was long and sharp. There was a long, bony crest on its head. The Indians had never seen a bird like it before.

So, the Sioux braves went back to their village with tales of this terrible bird—the Thunderbird as they called it, the mighty spirit who brought thunder.[5]

The thunderstones referred to in this story were cone-shaped fossilized shells. Because they looked like weapons, many ancient peoples worldwide believed they were thunderbolts thrown out of the stormy sky.

Other tribes who followed the buffalo across the Great Plains would have included the Arapaho, Arikara, Assiniboine, Blackfoot, Comanche, Cheyenne, Crow, Gros Ventre, Hidatsa, Ioway, Kaw, Kiowa, Kitsai, Missouria, Mandan, Omaha, Osage, Otoe, Pawnee, Plains Ojibwe, Plains Cree, Plains Apache, Ponca, Quapaw, Sarcee, Sioux, Stoney, Tonkawa, and Wichita.

These nomadic tribes would likely have passed through the Niobrara Chalk formations in western Kansas. The chalk beds first became famous when they were studied by a Yale University expedition led by Othniel Charles Marsh in 1870. The team recorded giant swimming reptiles called mosasaurs and plesiosaurs, the flying pterosaurs, clams up to six feet in diameter, and many types of smaller marine animals. Viewing the *Pteranodon* and mosasaur fossils together likely influenced or reinforced legends about the endless conflict between water monsters and Thunderbirds.

Although *Mosasaurus* species varied in length, some grew to be over 50 feet long. The longest mosasaur found in Kansas was about 40 feet long. Mosasaurs had long bodies, sharp teeth, and paddle-like limbs.

FUN FACT: All but six states have state fossils. Kansas, which was once covered by an ancient seabed, has two official state fossils: *Tylosaurus*, a swimming reptile, and *Pteranodon*, a flying reptile.

THE CROW

Originally from the Northeast, the Crow Tribe consists of two main bands. The River Crows originally lived along the Missouri, Milk, and Yellowstone Rivers in Montana and Wyoming. The Mountain Crows dwelt in the high mountains of northern Wyoming and southern Montana. The Crow Indian Reservation, defined in 1885, covers two and a half million acres southeast of Billings, Montana.

The Crow referred to the Thunderbird as Suadagagay. *Sua* means thunder and *dagagay* means bird. The Thunderbird is regarded as the most powerful of all spirits. Legend tells that the Thunderbird brings storms. Lightning zaps from his eyes when he blinks and thunder roars when he flaps his wings. If a Thunderbird strikes a human, it is because he is young and has not mastered his skill. Old Thunderbirds are wise and kill no one. They protect people who believe in them and offer them good fortune.

BRAVE WOLF AND THE THUNDERBIRD—A CROW LEGEND

One day, while Brave Wolf was out hunting, a large Thunderbird picked him up and carried him back to her nest. She pleaded for his help to stop the water serpent who lived in the lake at the bottom of the cliffs. She said every spring the monster would climb the cliff face and eat her babies.

Brave Wolf thought for a while, and then instructed the Thunderbird to bring him dry logs, round stones, and the hide of a large buffalo. The Thunderbird did as he said. Brave Wolf told the bird he would also need water but to wait until he told her to make it rain.

When the day came for the serpent to rise out of the water, Brave Wolf told the Thunderbird to bring rain, and she did, filling the basket Brave Wolf made from the buffalo hide. Brave Wolf built a fire and placed the stones within the flames. When the serpent climbed to the top of the cliffs, the Thunderbird struck it with lightning to no avail. The serpent kept climbing.

When it reached the top, the monster opened its mouth to devour the hatchlings, but Brave Wolf was waiting and tossed red hot stones into the creature's mouth. When the monster had swallowed all of them, Brave Wolf poured in the water. The water monster flailed and screamed then fell off the cliff and died. After a great feast, the Thunderbird carried Brave Wolf back home.

The Great Lakes Region

As early colonial America settled in to battle for its independence, patriotism even found its way into fossil gathering. In 1766, Count George-Louis Leclerc Buffon, French naturalist and curator of the King's Natural History Cabinet, proposed his "Theory of American Degeneracy" in Volume V of his highly popular work titled *Histoire Naturelle*. In this, he declared all living and once living creatures in the New World were inferior to those in Europe because of North America's cold, wet climate. This did not sit well with statesman Thomas Jefferson, who set out to prove the naturalist wrong.

In 1797, after Jefferson became president of the American Philosophical Society, he and other members of the group set out to procure a fossilized skeleton of a mastodon. When he became president, Jefferson commissioned the Corps of Discovery and instructed Meriwether Lewis and William Clark to be on the lookout for herds of mastodons. Of course, none were found, reinforcing the idea of inferiority that Jefferson had hoped to dispel.

After Lewis and Clark returned, Thomas Jefferson sent General Clark on a second assignment to inquire specifically about a mastodon found in a salty, sulfurous area along the Ohio River in Kentucky. In a letter dated 1807 December 19, Jefferson writes:

> I have lately received a letter from General Clarke. He has employed ten laborers several weeks, at the Big Bone Lick, and has shipped the result, in three large boxes, down the Ohio, via New Orleans, for this place, where they are daily expected. He has sent, 1st, of the Mammoth, as he calls it . . . 2d, of what he calls the Elephant . . . 3d, of something of the Buffalo species . . . There is a tusk and a femur which General Clarke procured particularly at my request, for a special kind of cabinet I have at Monticello.[6]

To prove that living things in the new world were not degenerate, Jefferson shipped some of these fossils to Europe. They were just as big as similar creatures found anywhere else in the world. In doing this, Jefferson may have been responsible for the attention and credibility paleontology received in the early nineteenth century. In 1866, financier and philanthropist George Peabody gave his nephew, Othniel Charles Marsh, his very own museum at Yale which resulted in the first professorship in paleontology in the United States. Marsh named and described a few of the most famous dinosaurs ever found: *Allosaurus, Apatosaurus* (*Brontosaurus*), *Diplodocus, Stegosaurus, Triceratops,* and several others.

The mastodon at Kentucky's Big Bone Lick may have been the first fossil discovery for the colonists in America, but it wasn't the first for Native Americans. Legends and myths about these giant relics had been circulating for centuries in the East just as they had in the West, with only slight variations.

THE OJIBWE

Also known as the Chippewa, the Ojibwe lived in the Michigan, Minnesota, Wisconsin, and North Dakota areas surrounding Lake Superior. Primarily hunters and fisherman, their version of the Thunderbird myth states he was created by Nanabozho, the great storytelling spirit, who was considered the master of life. Thunderbird's purpose was to counteract the underwater creature Manito who made rapids, caused stormy waters, tipped canoes, and chased away the fish. Each year, Thunderbird arrived with other birds in the spring and stayed through the season when underwater Manito posed the greatest danger.

Thunderbird also punished immoral humans. The Ojibwe made offerings to show respect for his power and to ask for success in hunting. They considered Thunderbirds to be powerful guardians who appeared in visions, and they also believed they accompanied the deceased into the afterworld

Furs, maple syrup, and bark from the birch tree were important products for the Ojibwe. The following legend tells how the birch tree obtained its burnt-black markings. One winter, a grandmother called to her grandson and said, "It is cold, and we have no fire for warmth or to cook with. Go west and find the Thunderbird's fire and bring it back for us." The grandson set out for the west, disguised as a little rabbit. When he finally reached Thunderbird's home, he said. "I am cold and lost. Will you please allow me to get warm?"

The Thunderbird agreed. Once inside, the little rabbit saw the fire and waited until Thunderbird looked away, then he quickly rolled in the fire and took off running toward his home with the fire on his back!

Thunderbird flew behind the rabbit throwing lightning flashes at him! Growing tired, the rabbit called for help. The birch tree, spoke. "Come, hide

The Ojibwe underwater spirit Manito was not entirely evil. He sometimes fed and sheltered those who fell into the icy waters of Lake Superior and offered medicinal powers to those who accepted him as their guardian. Without the spirit's aid or tolerance, the people believed they would starve or die in the temperamental waters of the Great Lake.

beside me my brother. I will protect you." The little rabbit hid beneath the tree while Thunderbird flashed and thundered. The lightning bolts missed the rabbit every time, but they hit the tree, leaving dark scars all over the bark. And that is why the birch tree looks as if it has burn marks.[7]

THE SHAWNEE

An Algonquian-speaking tribe, the Shawnee were the original inhabitants of modern-day Ohio, but they were a far-ranging people with villages located as far north as New York State and as far south as Georgia. Their name translates to "Southerners." The Shawnee followed animal populations throughout the winter months and established more permanent villages during the summers. Women gathered wood and tended to crops, while the men hunted and fought in battles. Villages or towns consisted of wigwams constructed from bundles of saplings covered with tree bark.

Shawnee legend tells of three figures that control weather. Grandmother Spirit created each of these. The first is Cyclone Person, a female spirit who causes tornadoes. The second is Four Winds whose colors the Shawnee call upon in prayer. The third and most popular weather spirit is Thunderbird, who causes it to storm when it fights with the Great Horned Serpent and other evil creatures. Lightning flashes from its eyes when it blinks. The Shawnee believe Thunderbirds guard the entrance to heaven. They honor them during the war dance as the patrons of war.

The Northeast

THE ABENAKI

Abenaki means "people of the dawn," or "easterners." Abenaki troops accompanied the French commander Charles LeMonyne de Longueui when he became the first European to encounter the mastodon fossils at Big Bone Lick in 1739. The Abenaki are the original natives of Vermont, New Hampshire, and Maine. After European colonists arrived, many Abenaki fled to Canada and became allies of the French. They lived in villages in small birchbark wigwams and sometimes erected log perimeters to ward off attackers. The neighboring Iroquois and Huron were violent enemies.

While culturally unique, tribes of the Northern Woodlands—including the Abenaki, Anishinabe, Wabanaki, Iroquois, Menominee, Cree, Lenape, Passamaquoddy, and Huron, among others—shared many of the same legends. The Woodland People considered the Thunderbird a powerful being and treated it with reverence, but they also believed it would rarely harm humans.

THE ORIGIN OF THE THUNDERBIRD: A PASSAMAQUODDY LEGEND

While this story can be found various places on the internet, we've paraphrased a version from *Indigenous Peoples Literature.*[8]

Two Indians desired to find the origin of thunder. They traveled north and came to a tall, magical mountain that drew apart and then snapped shut. The two jumped through, but one did not make it and was crushed.

On the other side, the surviving Indian came upon several Indians playing ball. He watched until they went inside their wigwams. Soon, they came out wearing costumes, carrying bows and arrows. They flew away over the mountains. This was how the Passamaquoddy Indian discovered where the Thunderbirds lived.

There were old men of the tribe remaining in the village, and they asked the lone traveler what he wanted. He said he wanted to learn where thunder came from.

After a time of deliberation, the elders said they would help him. They placed the Indian in a large mortar and pounded him until they broke all of his bones. They molded him into a new body with wings like Thunderbird and then sent him home, warning him not to fly too fast and risk injury.

Wochowsen, a great bird from the south, was jealous and wanted to be better than Thunderbird. Some time before, the Passamaquody hero Glooscap had broken Wochowsen's wings because of his reckless use of his power. On the night the Thunderbirds turned the lone Indian into one of them, Wochowsen created a horrible wind which was made even worse by his broken wings.

The air and sea became rancid, and all the fish died. The new Thunderbird called on Glooscap to repair Wochowsen's wings so the horribly strong winds would alternate with the calm, offering balance.

Legend tells us this is how the new Passamaquoddy Thunderbird—the lone Indian who passed through the cleft—became great and powerful. He was respected because he looked out for the good people.[9]

The American Southeast

THE CHOCTAW

The Choctaw occupy a large area of the southeastern United States, predominately in the Mississippi Valley. Their language belongs to the Muskogean family group.

One Choctaw tale reveals how thunder and lightning came to be. The Great Sun Father wanted to give his children a warning before he sent a storm. He called on a pair of large birds and said he would give them a home on top of the clouds if they would help warn his people of incoming storms. The people say that when the female lays her eggs on the clouds, they roll and make a loud noise. In his haste to catch the eggs, the male streaks across the sky so fast, he leaves a trail of lightning. The people recognized the birds' behaviors along with the rumbling and lightning, which the Great Sun Father thought was a good warning. This is why rain occurs with thunder and lightning.[10]

The American Southwest

While stories of the Thunderbird and water monsters in the Northwest and Northeast share a common emphasis on the elemental battle between nature and man; the southwest legends share a more sinister theme that involves giant birds swooping down with little warning and carrying off people. Whether the Pueblo people base these stories on fossil skeletons or actual happenings as told in the petroglyphs and drawings on pottery, no one knows for sure. But they entice one to ask an interesting question: Did *Pteranodon*s coexist alongside man in the American Southwest?

FUN FACT: *Pteranodon* means "wing without tooth." Most of the fossil remains of this creature come from the Smoky Hill Chalk of western Kansas. The first *Pteranodon* was discovered by O. C. March in 1870.

Pteranodon. ©Valentyna Chukhlyebova/ Shutterstock Image.

THE YAQUI

The Yaqui or Yoeme are an Uto-Aztecan speaking indigenous people of Mexico who inhabit the valley of the Río Yaqui in the Mexican state of Sonora and the southwestern United States. They also have communities in Chihuahua, Durango, and Sinaloa. The Pascua Yaqui Tribe live in Tucson, Arizona.

The Yaqui people speak of a giant bird that lived on the hill of Otan Kawi. Every morning it would fly out to capture human prey, carrying it off to Skeleton Mountain. The bird was impossible to kill due to its keen eyesight and ability to fly high in the sky. After many deaths, a young boy who had lost his family to the creature set out to kill it. An old villager suggested he hide among the bones of its victims that littered the hillside and ambush the bird. The boy did this and killed the creature with his bow and arrows. Legend states the feathers of the bird transformed into all the birds we see today, and the flesh became present-day animals and predators with claws. Now, only the bones of the bird remain on the hillside.[11]

THE PIMA IN ARIZONA AND THE SONORAN DESERT

While exploring the Sonoran Desert on February 12, 1699, Captain Juan Mateo Manje, an officer with the Spanish Army, was told by the Pima that a giant monster had once lived in a nearby cave. It had been a menace to the people because it would fly around and catch as many as it could eat.

One day, after the creature had eaten its fill, some of the people followed it back to its cave. When it was sound asleep, they closed the entrance with wood and set it on fire. The creature wasn't able to escape and died, asphyxiated by the smoke.

THE HOPI

Also an Uto-Aztecan tribe, the Hopi were villagers and farmers known for stock breeding, weaving, and creating pottery. They lived in two-story adobe homes in northern Arizona. Each Hopi village was divided into clans, governed by a chief who served as the spiritual leader.

The Hopi Pueblos are close to the ruins of Puerco Pueblo and Petrified Forest National Park, where a petroglyph of a large bird holding a struggling man in its long beak has been chiseled on a sandstone boulder. Adrienne Mayor, historian and author of *Fossil Legends of the First Americans*, asked about the image. She was told this picture depicted "a giant bird that used to swoop down on the pueblos and fly away with their children."[12]

Mel Cabre depiction of the petroglyph at the Puerco Pueblo ruins in Petrified Forest National Park.

The Jersey Devil

The Jersey Devil is a folktale that does not have roots in Native American legend or in another country. The creature was born in the late seventeenth and early eighteenth centuries as colonial Quakers settled into a wilderness of boundless opportunity. Perhaps American pride and a rigid version of patriotism thrust this creature into the limelight, but beneath the campfire stories and pop-culture allure there exists a very real monster.

Born during a time of religious upheaval, the Jersey Devil not only represented evil but unwelcome consequences that accompanied the Age of Enlightenment. Individualized thinking forced a progression that blurred traditional lines of good and evil and threatened the maintenance of set orders and values. This newfound freedom bred ever more forward thinking—and equally strong resistance.

With Puritans holding the positions of authority, individuals in the new Quaker territories of Pennsylvania and New Jersey faced persecution from their friends and neighbors. Being pacifists, Quaker overt responses to these persecutions were restrained, but they were just as quick as the Puritans to judge those who strayed from their beliefs.

Why? Was it to create a good society? To gain power before other belief systems took hold? Was this back and forth struggle between the ideals and beliefs of men and women a struggle for individualized independence in early America or a spiritual war, invisible to the human eye, yet reflected in legends and behavior?

Stories from the Lenape (Delaware) People, who had lived in and around the New Jersey Pine Barrens region for thousands of years, reinforced settlers' natural suspicion that an evil entity existed in the remote areas of the forest. This idea, combined with the belief systems of various immigrants, gave rise to three versions of the story that have grown and twisted, branching into a variety of modern tales that point back to the Jersey Devil. But before we dive into those three legends, we need to establish some historical context.

The Swedes, the Finns, and the Dutch

The first Europeans in the New Jersey area were the Swedes (along with a few Finns) and the Dutch, who set up trading centers along the Delaware River in the early 1600s. The earliest Dutch settlement was Fort Nassau in 1623. Because they positioned this city to the north and on the east side of the Delaware River, it was not easily accessible to those coming from the west, and the Dutch fur trade did not prosper so well. Today this is known as Gloucester City.

Conversely, the Swedes had built their settlement to the south and west side of the river. New Sweden, also known as Fort Christina, thrived at the edge of the wilderness near the mouth of the Delaware Bay until 1651, when the Dutch moved downriver and cut off their trading routes from the west. By 1655, the Swedes had relinquished control of their garrison, but the settlement of New Sweden remained.

With the addition of Fort Christina, the Dutch territory of New Netherland stretched from Albany, New York, in the north to Delaware in the south. The area encompassed parts of what are now the states of New York, New Jersey, Pennsylvania, Maryland, Connecticut, and Delaware.

FUN FACT: The first log cabin in America was built at Fort Christina by Swedish settlers sometime between 1638 and 1655.

©ehrlif/Shutterstock Image.

The Lenape

The Lenape people lived in an area they called *Lenapehoking*, which means "land of the Lenape." This territory covered what is now New Jersey, eastern Pennsylvania, southeastern New York State, northern Delaware, and a small section of southeastern Connecticut. The southernmost part of their lands teamed with wildlife—cougar, bear, deer, rabbit, turkey, wild cranberries, huckleberries, and strawberries. The Lenape often passed through this area—now known as the Pine Barrens—as they migrated to the coast to harvest shellfish.

The Lenape were a peaceful tribe who lived in groups mostly comprised of extended family. They lived in longhouses, farmed, and traded furs for European goods. They also shared the natural resources of the land.

In his journals, Johan de Laet, director of the Dutch West India Company, compiled a work of various writings on New Netherland and the encounters between the Dutch settlers and the Native Americans. De Laet described the Lenape as agreeable so long as they were treated fairly. Of their belief system he wrote:

> They have no sense of religion, no worship of God; indeed, they pay homage to the devil, but not so solemnly nor with such precise ceremonies as the Africans do. They call him in their language *Menutto* or *Menetto*, and whatever is wonderful and seems to exceed human capacity, they also call *Menetto*.[13]

The English and the Quakers

In 1664, the English arrived in New Netherland to claim the land they said John Cabot explored in 1497. Actually, Cabot would have made the trip in 1498, if he made it at all. Italian-born Cabot had worked for the English crown. Records indicate he landed in Newfoundland in 1497 and set out to explore the area to the south in 1498, but he mysteriously disappeared. No one knows if he made it to the area that became New Netherland, but no one could prove he hadn't explored the territory.

Regardless of whether their claims to ownership were valid, the English possessed a bigger Navy and forced the Dutch to surrender. King Charles II named Richard Nicoll, commander of the English fleet, as the first royal governor of the New York colony. He also renamed the area west of the Hudson River "New Jersey," after the island of Jersey in the English Channel. He gave all of this territory to his brother, James, the Duke of York.

Unbeknownst to the governor, who had parceled out the land to Puritan immigrants, James gave New Jersey to two of his friends—Lord John Berkeley and Sir George Carteret. Sir George appointed his brother Philip governor of New Jersey, and conflicts with the Puritans over political and religious differences were set in motion.

In 1674, Berkeley sold his share of the colony to two Quakers—Edward Byllynge and John Fenwick. A dispute between these two arose when Fenwick wanted more than his fair share. They both ended up financially bankrupt until a respected thirty-two-year-old William Penn and a few other Quakers bailed them out in 1676. Surveyors divided New Jersey into east and west halves and drafted a new deed. Carteret retained control over East New Jersey. Byllynge, William Penn, and other invested Quaker Friends retained control of West New Jersey.

Penn returned to England, but, with the help of Byllynge, he intended to establish the new colony of Burlington. They arranged transportation for 230 Quakers to arrive from Europe in 1677. Conflict with the Colonial English government arose as Sir Edmund Andros, the governor of the Province of New York, denied Byllynge authority to govern the western region of New Jersey. This created hardship for the newly arrived Quakers who were denied liberty, charged excessive taxes, and persecuted for their Quaker beliefs.

Byllynge wrote to Penn and explained their conflict. Penn drafted a charter of liberties for the settlement and sent it to King Charles. This contract provided for free counsel, trial by jury, freedom of conscience or religion, and more participatory and egalitarian elections.

Penn's document worked, and the king granted Byllynge (or whomever Penn and affiliates appointed) governmental control over West New Jersey, but not before winter set in. Construction on the new settlement hadn't yet started and the new colonists were about to freeze and starve. Byllynge garnered much needed help from the Lenape, who taught the settlers how to construct wigwams for shelter. The Swedes and Finns also assisted by providing food and other supplies. In a sad twist of fate, while the colony of Burlington flourished over the next five years, many of the Lenape who had helped them died from a smallpox epidemic.

William Penn. Quakers played an important role in the abolition of slavery and advancement of equal rights for women. They promoted education, nonviolence, and humane treatment of prisoners and the mentally ill. They also played a significant role in bringing about the Industrial Revolution. ©Morphart Creation/Shutterstock Image.

The Pine Barrens

Living in close proximity with the Lenape, the Dutch, Swedes, and English listened to stories about their forest spirit, Mising. This important deity is the protector of all animals of the forest but is most strongly associated with deer. The Lenape described Mising as a talking humanoid, riding through the woods on the back of a deer, helping respectful hunters and punishing those who harm the forest. The Mising were also sometimes described as deerlike beings with wings.

Kimochene, or nightwalkers, were witches that lived in the Pine Barrens and could fly, conjure spells, and travel great distances at night. The Lenape believed these nightwalkers were humans who inhabited the bodies of evil creatures. The Lenape didn't believe in the devil, but they believed in evil spirits. They paid homage to good spirits to keep the bad spirits away. While they spent a difficult winter together, one can assume the English and Lenape swapped stories surrounding their beliefs and customs.

As the English settled in at Burlington, a fear of witchcraft and devil worship moved throughout all of New England. The government had already passed a law in East New Jersey that any person found to be a witch would be put to death. Less formally, anyone behaving outside acceptable social and political norms would be treated with skepticism and likely deemed evil. It's probable the Quakers also associated Mising and other ominous stories about Pine Barrens creatures with evil, as they fell outside of their Christian beliefs. The setting was ripe for the emergence of a legend.

Quaker Persecution

In other parts of New England, Quakers were being persecuted much like they had been in England. Nearly fifteen thousand were jailed in England between 1660 and 1685. In the new world, the government (comprised mostly of Puritans) imprisoned 64 Quakers and lashed two 139 times, leaving one "beat like into a jelly." Another individual had been branded with the letter H, for heretic, after being whipped with thirty-nine stripes, and three Quakers were executed. Much of this discord had to do with the equality Quakers afforded women of the church, their unusual religious practices, and their intolerance for violence.[14]

An early convert to Quakerism—and a friend of the religion's founder, George Fox—William Penn also faced imprisonment and persecution for his beliefs. He was spared harsh treatment in the British judicial system because of his father's service as an admiral in the Royal Navy. In fact, on March 4, 1681, King Charles II granted William Penn a parcel of land west and south of New Jersey as compensation for his late father's work while serving the crown. Penn invited immigrating Quakers to live in the new colony he called Sylvania, which the King later called Pennsylvania to honor William's late father.

Subject only to the King, Penn drafted a democratic system similar to his charter of liberties. This granted full freedom of religion, fair trials, election of representatives, and a separation of powers—ideas that later formed the basis of the American constitution. During his residence in Pennsylvania from 1682 to 1684, Penn mapped out Philadelphia, the City of Brotherly Love, and invited Quakers and other repressed sects to take up residence in the surrounding areas of Pennsylvania, Delaware, and New Jersey. During this same time period, Penn and eleven other Quakers also purchased East New Jersey.

With all of his land holdings, William Penn became the largest non-monarchical landholder in the world. And he opened up another territory where the repressed could seek refuge—New Jersey became a land of diversity, a melting pot, founded on the principles of Quaker equality. But still, not everyone was accepted.

Where There Is Good, Evil Exists

We find the origins of the Jersey Devil entangled with three very different stories of intolerance that ultimately show how good intentions can inflict harm. The following stories are based in truth, but, as with any legend, time has a way of distorting the facts. We've taken care to report objectively the findings surrounding the three Jersey Devil theories. And remember that before there was a Jersey Devil, the creature was known as the Leeds Devil. The Leeds family contributed much to New Jersey history, and there are still many relatives of this large family living in the area today.

THEORY ONE: DANIEL LEEDS AND THE QUAKERS

Daniel Leeds was born in England on November 15, 1651. At age twenty-five, after the death of his first wife, Daniel and his brothers traveled to America, possibly with their father who settled in the New Jersey port city of Shrewsbury in 1677. Daniel, William, and Thomas stopped in Shrewsbury for a short time, but then traveled on to Burlington, New Jersey.

The year was 1678 when they arrived. The family business had been barrel making, but in this new world, Daniel's ambition met with great opportunity. William Penn and other prominent Quaker leaders wanted to turn the Delaware River valley into a thriving community of diverse people who lived free of persecution. Daniel was eager to help make that happen. He apparently worked as a cooper (barrel maker) for a short time, farmed, and served in the local assembly, soon rising to the rank of gentleman.

A religious man, Daniel grew up Anglican but converted to Quakerism as it allowed for a deeper, more personal experience with God. In Burlington, Daniel attended meetings regularly and donated money to help build the Burlington Friends Meeting House that still stands to this day.

Fascinated by the writings of German philosopher Jacob Boehme, Daniel entertained ideas of Christian mysticism in which divine illuminations, visions, and altered states of consciousness were part of the Christian experience. As the Age of Enlightenment took hold, aspiring intellectuals like Daniel embraced new ways of thinking. He took up the study of astrology to benefit everyday life and began to make calculations and predictions associated with weather and health issues.

Life away from the formalities of society allowed the Quakers to avoid persecution, but the hard work and limited contact with others sheltered them from the latest news and educational opportunities. Daniel felt a responsibility to broaden the community's scope of knowledge. In 1687, he developed New Jersey's first almanac—the *American Almanac*. He teamed up with printer and fellow Quaker William Bradford to produce a one-page sheet that offered weather forecasts, tide tables, and best planting dates for farmers. As was customary, he used astrological calculations.

Not long before, the church had warned Bradford not to print unapproved material. But he ignored them and agreed to print the Leeds almanac, knowing the language and astrological references would offend the church. Even though Daniel intended the almanac for the community at-large, Quaker elders ordered all circulating copies be gathered up and destroyed. They also required Daniel to apologize publicly for offending the church. He did so, but not without humiliation.

To convey his faith and share what he felt were important truths to the other intellects within the community, Daniel wrote and compiled *The Temple of Wisdom for the Little World, in Two Parts*. This 200+ page philosophical book was about origins, divine mysteries of man and the universe, and moralities. It contained prayers, poems, and other writings that supported Daniel's way of thinking. William Bradford printed it in 1688—the first book printed in New Jersey. It met with instant criticism. The Quaker church gathered up and destroyed almost every copy, even those that came directly off the press in London.

By this time, Daniel had acquired the position of deputy surveyor and garnered the respect of nonreligious people in the community. In 1694, he left the Quaker church. It was also the year he surveyed a plot of land in present-day Galloway Township and called it Leeds Point. He built a house to serve as the Leeds family homestead and set up his oldest son Japheth to live in it, but Daniel continued to live and serve in Burlington County. He and William Bradford proceeded to publish a more traditional twenty-one-page almanac booklet as well as other works that attacked the Quaker religion.

About this time, the once-zealous Quaker missionary George Keith also turned against the Quaker church, believing they had strayed from their original faith. He stirred up major controversy and received criticism in the form of an anti-Keithian pamphlet written by church elder and Philadelphia assemblyman, Caleb Pusey. Daniel joined Keith's cause and used his talent for the written word to answer Caleb Pusey with an anti-Quaker pamphlet, defending Keith and himself.

In 1697, Daniel wrote *The Trumpet Sounded Out of the Wilderness of America*. In it, Leeds said Quaker theology denied the divinity of Jesus. He also accused the Quakers of being anti-monarchists, which was probably not far from the truth. For several years, the people of Pennsylvania and New Jersey had been living without a structured government and enjoyed it.

While Daniel had risen to the esteemed position of surveyor general and acted as a judge within the county, he identified as a British loyalist. He became increasingly unpopular when he served on the council of Crown-appointed governor Edward Hyde, also known as Lord Cornbury. Fully aware of the people's desire to distance themselves from the monarchy, Daniel lied about the vote count, ensuring Britain retained majority control of the council.

In 1700, Quaker Caleb Pusey attacked Leeds personally, writing, "Satan's Harbinger Encountered . . . Being Something by Way of Answer to Daniel Leeds." Pusey had now publicly accused Daniel of being evil. Could this be where the origin of the Leeds Devil began? With Daniel Leeds, his wayward belief system, and the slanderous accusations of the Quaker church? If so, it's only half the story.

By 1714, Daniel Leeds was ready to retire from the back and forth diatribes and political maneuvering. He turned the almanac over to his sons and coached from the background. When Daniel died in 1720, his youngest son Titan continued publishing the *American Almanac*. But in 1732, a twenty-six-year-old Boston native who'd recently moved to Philadelphia also entered the almanac-publishing foray.

A man with unlimited ambition, Benjamin Franklin was also a great marketer whose confidence and optimistic mindset made him an oppositional nightmare for Titan Leeds. When Franklin decided to publish an almanac under the pseudonym of Poor Richard Saunders, he knew how to use his wit and humor to push a few of Titan Leeds's buttons.

Intelligent and informed, Franklin knew all about Titan's father and his involvement with George Keith and Lord Cornbury. He also knew his competition still used astrology, a topic the predominantly Quaker community still opposed. Using his famously witty and entertaining writing style, Benjamin Franklin debuted *Poor Richard's Almanac* in 1733 by predicting Titan Leeds death using astrological calculations. Poking fun at Leeds, Franklin wrote (with some corrections applied for ease of reading) of his concern about competing with his fellow author,

> Mr. Titan Leeds, whose interest I was extremely unwilling to hurt; but this obstacle (I am far from speaking it with pleasure) is soon to be removed, since inexorable death, . . . has already prepared her mortal Darts. . . . He dies, by my calculation made at his request, on October 17, 1733, 3:29 p.m., at the very instant of the conjunction of the Sun and Mercury; by his own calculation he will survive till the 26th of the same month. This small difference between us we have disputed whenever we met these nine years past. . . . Which of us is most exact, a little time will now determine. As therefore these Provinces may no longer expect to see any of his Performances after this year, I think myself free to take up the task.[15]

Titan did not see the humor in the prediction of his death. While he rebutted Franklin, he was not, like his father, a savvy businessman who could spin words into gold. Titan stopped publishing the *American Almanac* in 1736, about the same time the Leeds Devil was supposedly born.

Even after Titan Leeds's death in 1738, Franklin continued his assault by writing letters as if they came from Leeds's ghost. Was this the seed that sprouted the legend of the Leeds Devil? Franklin would have been one to spin a good yarn.

THEORY TWO: MOTHER LEEDS

The roots of this story are thought to be in the family of Daniel Leeds's old-est son, Japheth (1682–1748) and his wife Deborah (1685–1748). The Leeds had twelve children, and they were the only family in the area to have such a large family. Their last child was born in 1726

Devout Quakers, Japheth and Deborah held meetings in their home. In 1706, circuit Quaker minister Thomas Chalkey documented an unfortunate encounter with Daniel Leeds and other backsliders. Everyone knew Daniel, and he was always the subject of controversy. As Chalkey came and went from Japheth Leeds's homestead, rumors would have surfaced about the "Leeds Devil." Who knows? Maybe later those rumors entwined with sto-ries about a thirteenth child born (or not) to the Leeds family on a stormy night in South Jersey.

There are several variations of the "Mother Leeds" story. The most pop-ular version states that in 1735, Mother Leeds became pregnant with her thirteenth child. Weary of motherhood, she cursed the child and said, "Let

it be a devil." After the baby was born, it morphed into a hideous creature, growing horns out of a horse-shaped head. The body elongated, sprouting leathery, bat-like wings. A long tail and claws emerged as back feet changed into cloven hooves. The beastly creature wailed loudly and flew up the chimney and out into the Pine Barrens, where some argue he continues to terrorize humans and feast on livestock today.

Other story variations have the creature eating the entire family before it flies out the window. Some say Mother Leeds kept the child hidden away because of deformities. Hiding developmentally disabled children was not an uncommon practice in the eighteenth century. And this leads to our third theory of the Jersey Devil's origin.

THEORY THREE: THE SHOURD WOMAN AND HER DEFORMED CHILD

As the lives of the Leeds men became engaged in religion and politics, an equally, if not more, ambitious venture was underway. When colonists first arrived in South Jersey, they called it "barren" because their crops would not grow in the sandy, acid soil. But on the surface of area lakes and ponds floated a thin film of rust. This iron oxide combined with sand and gravel to form a low-grade iron ore that gathered along the stream banks. Workers mined the rivers, retrieving ore masses of various sizes and hauling them to the furnaces. The first iron furnace in New Jersey was established in Tinton Falls, Monmouth County, before 1684. Out of necessity, Charles Read built Batsto Ironworks in 1766. Batsto shipped cast-iron water pipes, stoves, axe heads, shovels, and pots and pans all over the eastern seaboard.

At one time, there were seventeen furnaces burning twenty-four hours a day until the rivers froze over. Many furnaces operated throughout the Revolutionary War, making, supplying, and housing munitions. Batsto and Hanover supplied cannon balls for Washington's armies during the revolution and also for the War of 1812.

Each iron furnace required thirty square miles of timber to make the charcoal necessary to operate the furnaces. Because of this, charcoal making was one of the first industries in the Pine Barrens. Sawmills also sprang up throughout the Pine Barrens, turning out lumber for houses and ships.

FUN FACT: In 1749, Benjamin Franklin urged forestry practices be enacted within the Pine Barrens and surrounding areas to avoid the "reckless and wanton slaughter of the woods."[16]

General store and post office at historical Batsto Village, New Jersey. ©Mel Cabre.

During the iron era, owners developed company towns near their furnaces to attract and keep workers. The communities often comprised employee homes, a gristmill, a post office, a general store, a school, and a church. Workers were often paid in store credit which kept them bound to their employer as they worked to pay off debt.

Unfortunately by 1820 most of the natural stores of bog iron had been depleted, and in the 1840s metallurgists in Pennsylvania discovered coal, which was much more efficient than charcoal, along with a richer source of iron. While industrialists turned toward glass and paper making, employment opportunities for the general laborer plummeted. Those who wanted to remain in the Pines turned to cultivating cranberries and blueberries, making charcoal, and harvesting other products used by florists and nurseries. Because of the loss of their major employers and the remoteness of the location, the people of the Pine Barrens lived simple lives divided between work and family. It is out of this hardworking, simple life in the remote Pine Barrens that our third Jersey Devil origin theory arises.

In 1913, Henry Goddard and Elizabeth Kite, a pair of psychologists working for the Vineland Training School for Feeble-Minded Boys and Girls, entered the Pine Barrens to trace the lineage of one of their residents named Deborah Kallikak (this is a false last name) to determine if feeble-mindedness was hereditary. After perusing genealogies and interviewing countless individuals, the psychologists wrote up their findings in a book called *The Kallikak Family: A Study of Heredity and Feeble-Mindedness*. The results of their study showed that Deborah and several other individuals in the Pine Barrens area who suffered from "feeble-mindedness" all originated with one man—Martin Kallikak.

Martin Kallikak had been a soldier in the colonial militia during the American Revolution. He had an affair with a young barmaid who became pregnant. The soldier moved on to live his life while the barmaid went on to have a son. This son grew up and inherited "his father's name and his mother's mental capacity." But he could live on his own. He worked as a laborer, built a crude home, married, and had ten children and many grandchildren, great-grandchildren, great-great-grandchildren, and great-great-great-grandchildren. One of these was Deborah Kallikak.

Henry Goddard's study became one of the most popular and highly publicized eugenics studies in America. The book was printed in Germany in 1914 and then reprinted in 1933, the same year Nazi Germany passed the "Law for Prevention of Offspring with Hereditary Defects Act."

The true story of the Kallikak family was deeply embellished to fit the political agenda of a popular movement, which was to raise awareness of eugenics and to justify the sterilization of people considered a drain on society. Later researchers found parts of Goddard's work to be fictitious and discredited the study. Even Goddard would eventually back away from his claims, having "reversed many of his early opinions, declaring in multiple public forums that he had been gravely mistaken in many of his most famous conclusions . . . [and] he frequently voiced his new opinion that feeble-minded people should be allowed to have children, if they choose to do so. . . . He never intended for his book to be connected with Hitler, Nazism, and the Holocaust."[17] But the work had left a mark on the Pine Barrens, painting the residents as poor, uneducated, feeble-minded people who drained the economy.

Which finally brings us to the story of Mrs. Shourds as told to Henry Charlton Beck, New Jersey folklore historian (an attribution given in his obituary) and author of several books about New Jersey, including *Jersey*

Genesis (1945). In the 1940s, a local resident had driven Henry Beck to the remains of the Shourd house at Leeds Point and revealed that a Mrs. Shourds, not a Mrs. Leeds, had given birth to the Jersey Devil at this location. She was the mother of twelve children and pregnant with her thirteenth. Some versions of the story state she dabbled in witchcraft and was so distraught by her pregnancy she cursed the baby. Sometime later, she gave birth to a deformed child that she kept hidden from the world.

According to Bill Sprouse, author of *The Domestic Life of the Jersey Devil or, Bebop's Miscellany* (2013), the deformed child theory seemed to be the consensus of many modern-day locals that he interviewed. Henry Beck conceded that it wasn't uncommon for parents to "hide" their disabled children from prying eyes. Who could blame them after what happened to Deborah Kallikak?

Many years before the Kallikak book was released, Daniel Leeds and his family had faded into the fine print of historical records. But with the help of a couple of journalists and writers, the Leeds Devil would morph into the Jersey Devil and become colonial America's original monster, forever haunting the Pine Barrens and the surrounding areas.

Introduction to the Legend of Mothman

The Mothman of Point Pleasant struggles to find its place in history as a cryptid. As we've seen with Thunderbird and the Jersey Devil, most legendary cryptids are born out of a cultural truth. Mothman does not appear to fit this pattern for unknown animals, aliens, or paranormal entities, although we'll talk more about how he might in the next chapter. For now, our goal is to focus on historical context.

Mothman first appeared in Point Pleasant in 1967 amid a frenzy of UFO sightings and thirteen months before the disastrous and deadly Silver Bridge collapse. While Mothman likely finds his roots in military operations and Cold War tactics, we want to go back farther into the past and explore stories surrounding the people who lived in and around Point Pleasant, West Virginia, to see if any connections can be made.

The most obvious place to start is with Hokoleskwa, more commonly known as Cornstalk, the principle chief of the Shawnee nation, who is said to have cursed the land around Point Pleasant in 1777, shortly prior to his death. The entire region had been wrought with fighting and loss long before the peacemaking chief was murdered, however, first between tribal nations and then between the Native Americans and early settlers. Is it possible a curse (or evil entity) existed long before Cornstalk's infamous murder? One that accompanies all human desire and selfishness? This is what we'll focus on as we talk about the history surrounding Mothman's appearance.

Out of the Past: A Generation of War in the Ohio Valley

In the year 1680, several hundred Shawnee Native Americans lived in the territory from Fort St. Louis on the Illinois River to as far south as Georgia and South Carolina. A large settlement also formed along the Tallapoosa River in Alabama, where they lived alongside the Creek Tribe, with whom they had formed an alliance. A nomadic people, the Shawnee followed and hunted game, raided other tribes, and traded with Europeans. They (and other tribes) found a profit in selling one another as slaves to the Europeans. The entirety of a generation grew up surrounded by territorial conflict.

When Thomas Chalkley—the same Quaker minister who had a run in with Daniel Leeds—visited an Indian council in 1706, he was surprised the Shawnee included women in their council meetings. In his diary, he recorded, "In the council was a woman who took a part in the deliberations of this council, as well as upon all important occasions. On the interpreter being questioned why they permitted a woman to take so responsible a part in their councils, he replied that some women were wiser than some men and that they had not done anything for years without the council of this ancient, grave woman, who spoke much in this council."[18] A major role of the Wise Woman was to help keep peace and prevent unnecessary bloodshed.

Into the next decade, Shawnees began moving to Pennsylvania and settling along the Delaware River. Because of Penn's Treaty, signed in 1683, the Shawnee experienced peace in the region, but they did not convert to Christianity like the Lenape. They maintained a wary eye, unable to fully trust the Europeans, who had introduced whiskey and taken advantage of their kindness. After Penn's death in 1717, relations between the Native Americans and the English settlers deteriorated.

Because they admired the diplomatic structure and organization of the Iroquois Confederacy, Crown officials invited the Iroquois nation to speak for the Shawnee and other tribes. This irritated the Shawnee, so they moved west into Ohio and West Virginia and began talking with the French. This made the new Pennsylvania governor nervous. He spoke with Shawnee delegates in 1739 to reaffirm the treaty. The Shawnee promised their loyalty to the British.

> **FUN FACT:** The Iroquois Confederacy—a political and cultural union among five Iroquoian speaking nations—was founded between 1450 and 1600 by Hiawatha, an Onondaga chief, and Deganawida, a Huron prophet adopted by the Mohawk. Their goal was to establish peace among warring tribes.

Colonel John Stuart, a chronicler of pioneer history and author of *Memoir of Indian Wars and Other Occurrences and Eyewitness Accounts of the American Revolution* (1799), called the Shawnee "the most bloody and terrible" of all Indians. He also considered that they were "a well-formed, active, and ingenious people . . . assuming and imperious in the presence of others, not of their own nation, and were sometimes very cruel."[19] Most Europeans who encountered the Shawnee on friendly terms, however, found the Shawnee talkative and cheerful. The Shawnee delighted in entertaining visitors who came to them with no hidden agenda.

Ignoring Native American interests, Britain and France both laid claim to America through their charters and discovery. Each believed whoever controlled the Ohio Valley would control the country. The Iroquois were astute in playing one nation against the other while continuing to act as the official spokesmen for all Native Americans. The local tribes of Shawnee, Miami, Wyandot, and Delaware (to name a few) also manipulated the rival nations to serve their personal goals.

The British proved they weren't allies of the Shawnee, however, when they refused to help them fight French bullying in 1750. They further alienated the Shawnee by declaring the Native Americans wouldn't inherit land. When the French and Indian War began in 1754, the Shawnee sided with the French. But they weren't winning and the war was costing them many lives.

In 1758, at Easton, Pennsylvania, the governors of Pennsylvania and New Jersey gathered with over five hundred tribal members of the Lenape, Shawnee, Iroquois, and ten other tribes. After a week of negotiations, they came to an agreement that the Native Americans would not fight on the side of the French, and, in return, Pennsylvania would return large blocks of land which the Iroquois had ceded years prior. The royal governors promised to recognize the Ohio River Valley as sacred hunting grounds and to avoid further colonial settlement west of the Allegheny Mountains after the war. They signed on these terms in the Treaty of Easton. With reinforced power from the homeland, British troops overran the French, occupied their forts, and built many of their own.

At the close of the French and Indian War in 1763, local colonists who cared little about Britain, France, or the terms of the treaty, moved into the Ohio territory. Adding insult to injury, the Shawnee received word that the Iroquois had "given" their land back to Britain.

The shady deal meant little to the tribes in the area—the Iroquois had no rights outside a battle that had taken place decades earlier. But in 1763, the Ottawa war chief Pontiac led a rebellion and overtook every British post west of the Appalachians except Fort Detroit. This became known as Pontiac's Rebellion, and it sparked other conflicts and skirmishes between the Native Americans and the Redcoats.

To avoid another war, the British Crown implemented the Royal Proclamation of 1763. This defined the Appalachian Mountains as the boundary line between Native American lands and colonial settlements. Only Crown-appointed officials and licensed traders were permitted west of the Appalachians. But still the settlers came. The back and forth fighting continued. Many people died.

Shawnee chief Charlot Kaske presented his clear understanding of the situation to approaching British troops not long after Pontiac's rebellion: "'You English, when you first came amongst us, only settl'd upon the Sea Coasts and ask'd for a very small quantity of land,' Charlot said. 'But as more and more of you came over and as you increased, you ask'd again for a span length and then for a step, which we poor Indians always gave you. Now you envy us every good spot of land we have, even for our hunting.'"[20]

In 1768, the British government proposed an amendment to the Proclamation of 1763. This agreement, called the Treaty of Stanwix, established a new boundary farther west, ceding most of West Virginia and Kentucky to Britain for colonial expansion. But negotiations took place between British crown officials and the Iroquois, not the colonists and the Shawnee. "'You think yourselves Masters of the Country,' said Nimwha, brother of Shawnee Chief Cornstalk. 'You have taken it from the French, who, as you know had no right to it, as it is the property of us Indians.'"[21]

Conflict continued as the Shawnee refused to sign the treaty, stating it was a plan concocted between the British and Iroquois to steal their lands. The Shawnee built a coalition of western Native American tribes that extended from the Great Lakes in the north to the Creek Nation in the south. Near the mouth of the Scioto River, they erected a large council house and held multi-tribal meetings there.

Colonists did not agree with the treaty either. Daniel Boone entered Native American territory in 1769 along with fur trader, John Finley, and a crew of Virginia trappers. The Shawnee tracked and captured Daniel and John, forcing them to reveal their campsite. After raiding the trappers' goods, the Shawnee in charge, Captain Will, gave each man a pair of moccasins and a gun. He told them, "Go home and stay there. Don't come here anymore, for this is the Indians' hunting ground, and all the animals, skins, and furs are ours; and if you are so foolish as to venture here again, you may be sure the wasps and yellow-jackets will sting you severely."[22]

But still the Virginians came. The Shawnee fought against colonial settlement until 1774. Area tribes, weary of the violence, opted to live in peace. They abandoned the Shawnee and left them to fight alone. In late October, Virginia governor, Lord Dunmore, led an army of 1,500 men down the Ohio River from Fort Pitt, while General Andrew Lewis led another militia group of near the same number down the Kanawha River.

Chief Cornstalk repeatedly urged his warriors to seek peace, but the young Shawnee would not listen. Cornstalk and the Shawnee war chiefs Black Hoof, Black Fish, Blue Jacket, and Puckeshinwa came together with their few remaining allies to launch an attack. Their numbers totaled a meager seven hundred men. At sunrise, they attacked Lewis's army

Tecumseh, Shawnee warrior chief. He assembled thousands of Shawnee to fight for Native American lands in the Ohio Valley.

Chief Cornstalk Memorial. Located in Tu Endie Wei State Park, Point Pleasant, West Virginia. ©2019 T. S. Mart.

at Fort Blair near a place called Point Pleasant. At first, the Shawnee rallied, but when Dunmore's force arrived, they overpowered the Shawnee and drove them back across the Ohio River. Several men died, including a young Tecumseh's father.

Colonel John Stuart, who fought at Point Pleasant, wrote of Cornstalk: "I could hear him the whole day speaking very loud to his men; and one of my company who had once been a prisoner, told me what he was saying; encouraging the Indians, telling them 'be strong, be strong!'"[23]

After the battle, Cornstalk was angry at the loss of life and at his young warriors who wanted to continue to fight. With the onset of the Revolutionary War, the British urged the Shawnee to help drive the American settlers out of the region. Several of the younger Shawnee warriors stopped listening to Cornstalk and left to join Governor Henry Hamilton at Fort Detroit to launch an attack on the colonial militia.

Cornstalk traveled to Fort Blair to warn the Americans. According to Colonel John Stuart, who was present at the fort, Cornstalk and those with him were taken hostage for fear of an ambush but were treated well. The chief even helped the Americans make maps and strategize against the British. But on November 10, 1777, when a soldier was shot outside the fort (presumably by a Shawnee, although this was never confirmed), embittered comrades stormed the fort and killed Cornstalk, his son, and a man named Red Hawk without warning.

A 1928 historical pageant found in an elementary school states that before he died, an angry chief Cornstalk uttered what has become known as "Cornstalk's Curse." Not known to be either fact or fiction, variations of the curse can be found across the internet and follow some variation of the following:

> I was the border man's friend. Many times I have saved him and his people from harm. I never warred with you, but only to protect our wigwams and lands. I refused to join your paleface enemies with the red coats. I came to the fort as your friend and you murdered me. You have murdered by my side, my young son. For this, may the curse of the Great Spirit rest upon this land. May it be blighted by nature. May it even be blighted in its hopes. May the strength of its peoples be paralyzed by the stain of our blood.[24]

Into the Present Under the Veil of a Curse

Colonel Stuart recorded Cornstalk's last words as: "'When I was a young man and went to war, I thought that might be the last time, and I would return no more. Now, I am here among you; you may kill me if you please; I can die but once; and it is all one to me, now or another time.'" About this speech, Stuart further adds, "This declaration concluded every sentence of his speech." An hour later Cornstalk was dead.[25]

There was likely no curse placed on the territory by Cornstalk. Not only was he a man of exceptional character, bent on living in peace, but he died instantly. With so many options to include in a school play, why would the author add a curse? Was it a way to rationalize the bad things that had happened in the community since 1777? Did people feel a need to blame someone for the hardships in their lives? Was there lingering animosity between white men and Native Americans? Regardless of the reason, people chose to believe. And when beliefs found confirmation in harsh realities, even misfortunes that any community might face, the curse received the power it needed to be blamed for all future hardships that fell on Pleasant Point and the surrounding area. That is why, in 1966, many believe evil entered the region and stayed there for thirteen months.

The Legend of Mothman and the Silver Bridge

It began on November 12, when five men digging a grave near Clendenin, West Virginia, reported they saw a figure fly overhead. Against the moonlit sky, it looked like a large, manlike bird. Three days later, two couples out for a drive near what the town of Point Pleasant called the TNT area—about six miles north of the town—said they saw a large gray creature with glowing red eyes. On first appearance, the creature had been caught in a wire. Not long after, the couples reported it appeared in front of their '57 Chevy, forcing them to stop. When the seven-foot creature spread his wings, the couples took off down Highway 62 toward home. The creature followed, topping speeds of 100 miles per hour.

Having lost the creature, the four stopped at the edge of town and regrouped, certain what they had seen was a bird. They went back to double check, and, as they neared the TNT plant, their headlights fell upon the thing as it stood beside the road, staring at them with large red eyes. Immediately, the figure spread its wings and lifted into the air.

At least eight more sightings followed in the next three days, along with a variety of bizarre occurrences—strange lights in the sky, power and TV glitches, missing dogs, hallucinations, and bouts of precognition. Those who encountered Mothman were left with a lingering sense of doom.

Some witnesses said strange Men in Black with pale, translucent skin visited them and asked for details about their lives. Then in flat, robotic tones, they warned them not to tell anyone about their encounters with Mothman. Other witnesses received strange phone calls in the same robotic voice with the same message.

Some area residents believed Mothman had taken up residence in an abandoned ammunitions facility that once made dynamite used during World War II. They thought his many encounters with humans were attempts to communicate the impending collapse of the Silver Bridge that took place on December 15, 1967, thirteen months after the first sighting. The tragedy caused thirty-one cars to fall into frigid water, killing forty-six people.

No one knows if Mothman was a demonic force that circled the area before tragedy struck, or a spirit gone rogue, crossing from the spiritual to the human realm, attempting to warn people. Are Men in Black part of a demonic clean-up crew, working to hush people up? Or a tall tale justifying a need for silence about elaborately played hoaxes?

UFOs, Men in Black, and strange lights were common occurrence across America in the 1950s and 1960s. Is it possible Mothman was one more story fabricated by UFO enthusiasts? Or was he part of a government tactic to divert attention away from the Cold War and experimental weapons testing?

Whatever Mothman is or isn't, he is here to stay in the world of cryptids, where fascination and curiosity run wild with a desire to understand and explain the unknown. For more on Mothman sightings in Chicago and Kentucky, see the Mothman profile in chapter 2. In chapter 4 we'll go into more depth about the ammunitions facility and the government's presence in Point Pleasant during and after World War II.

4

SKY MONSTER CULTURE

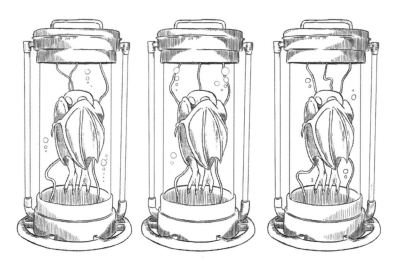

A Culture of Belief

One trait that differentiates humans from animals is the ability to nurture and articulate our beliefs. Several definitions for the word belief exist, but for the subject of this book we'll go with the second definition offered by Merriam-Webster online: "a belief is something that is accepted, considered to be true, or held as an opinion." Belief systems are complex and individual, but core ideas are often shared by a larger group. Beliefs are an expression of acquired and sifted knowledge.

At the core of human behavior is a belief system. Systems are groups of things that work together, creating a whole. The human digestive system is a good example. The mouth, digestive juices, stomach, and intestines, along with a few other body parts all work together to extract nutrients from food and dispose of waste.

Our belief systems are similar. We gain knowledge (food) from the world, sift through and interpret (digest) it, and either store it, use it (nutrients, fat, energy, etc.), or do both. Unlike the systems in our physical bodies, though, the belief system can be altered as we acquire more knowledge, usually through the influence of important people or relationships.

We are not born with a belief system. As infants, we begin to learn, through observation and the influence of trusted adults, to interpret information in our environment. When we start school, our interpretation of earlier ideas continues to change, influenced by others, such as our peers and our teachers, whose opinions matter to us. Our personalities also begin to dictate our ideas and influencers. Personality develops as a person learns how to use and manipulate her perception of the world. Everyone's personality differs because we combine unique biological factors with equally distinct social histories and environments. Belief systems also continue to evolve, because they are a product of the individual, the knowledge they pursue and obtain, societal and family influences, and their evolving personality and behaviors.

Becoming Legends

Our belief systems shape our worldviews. In its simplest terms, a worldview is the lens we look through to interpret everything around us, including cryptids. When confronted with more than one plausible interpretation, we always interpret evidence in a manner consistent with how we already see the world. It's important to ask ourselves and others basic questions about theology, philosophy, ethics, biology, sociology, psychology, law, politics, economics, and history. Understanding where our beliefs and assumptions in these areas originate helps us to productively engage with one another's worldviews.

In this book, our goal is to give a broad overview of sky monsters and how different belief systems have turned these cryptids into legends. We're not interested in preaching or indoctrinating. But because of our worldview, we write in a family-friendly style and observe the world as a creation. So, when we talk about extinct *Pteranodons*, we'll remain open to the possibility they lived at the same time as humans, even though many scientists dispute this. It's also important for us to present observational evidence like fossils and petroglyphs without making assumptions.

While searching for a theme to this book, we were surprised to find commonalities among the Thunderbird, the Jersey Devil, and Mothman. These cryptids are not legends because of pop culture or modern-day sightings, but because each has been woven into the American fabric by deep, long-standing belief systems: the Thunderbird by Native American philosophy and spirituality, the Jersey Devil by Quaker and Puritan beliefs, and Mothman by anxieties about government secrecy and a Cold War mindset. These are huge topics to which authors have devoted complete books. We will focus solely on belief systems as they relate to these flying cryptids. Here are a few characteristics of all belief systems that will become evident as we dive into individual cultures:

- They have boundaries that when crossed set off alarms in our minds. This is our conscience nudging us to pay attention and be careful.
- They serve a purpose to help us navigate life.
- They create comfortable environments for sharing ideas among group members.
- Networks of influence and support develop as people with common interests come together.

The Thunderbird

Legend Gives Way to Logic

Native American beliefs find their roots in nature and the interpretation of the natural world. While there are no written, foundational texts, there is a universal belief in an overarching power that created everything. Belief systems about this divine power vary from one tribe to another and may include elements of pantheism, or the inclusion of many gods as one god. They may also include animism, or the idea that humans, animals, and meaningful aspects of our environment, sometimes even inanimate objects, contain a purpose and essence beyond their physical existence. A few names for the overarching divine power among Native Americans include *Wakan Tanka* (Sioux), *Tam Apo* (Shoshone), *Gitche Manitou* (Algonquian-speaking tribes), and *Raweno* (Iroquoian-speaking nation). This deity was called *Tabaldak* by the Abenaki and *Kishelemukong* by the Lenape.

Native Americans and other indigenous people perceive the universe as a living entity that nurtures all life, and desire to preserve it more than cultures who seek to develop natural resources. Goals are embedded in a belief system that values observation and preservation of the natural world and maintaining harmony between the earth and people; the focus is not on obtaining personal salvation or liberation. In Native American belief systems, in the face of new information and understanding, legend often incorporates or gives way to logic.

Beliefs in magic, signs, and omens are common. Many believe animals possess magical powers and can serve as guardian spirits. Incantations and the offering of gifts or sacrifices shows respect for the guardian spirit and can allow one to remain in its favor.

Rituals and ceremonies focus on important aspects of life such as hunting, agriculture, war, weather, and family. They allow one to seek the help of a higher and stronger power. Thunderbird is one such power: he can protect the people and bring rain and sustenance to the land.

To explain or justify hardship, Native Americans might believe they have offended the supernatural powers. A person whose home or field has been struck by lightning, or whose crops have been flooded, may need to seek favor with Thunderbird by offering small sacrifices, performing individual ceremonies, or openly apologizing. Reparation varies by tribe and tradition.

Native Americans attach symbolic meaning to elements of nature to portray their way of life. Symbols used on bodies, clothes, homes and weapons include geometric representations of celestial bodies, natural phenomena, and animals. War paint and tattoos used by Indian warriors also held sacred meaning.

The Thunderbird represents power, protection, and strength. We see evidence for this in the previous section, where he is almost always a dominant force associated with weather or other natural phenomenon. While his anger can lead to punishment, Thunderbird is an unbeatable fighting spirit who also represents courage, abundance, and prosperity.

The Jersey Devil

Intolerance Births Monsters

Throughout the scriptures, the Bible equates witchcraft with casting spells, sorcery, and the summoning or consulting of the dead. So why were thousands of people put to death for only having a strange birthmark, a mental illness, living alone, or cultivating medicinal herbs? How did this happen?

From the earliest mention of witchcraft in chapter 28 of book 1 Samuel of the Bible, men of power have manipulated the biblical definition to serve whatever cause best fits their needs. Two hundred years before the Pilgrims arrived in America, witch trials were held in Switzerland, in the southern region of Valais, where at least 367 men and women were put to death. In 1486, James Sprenger and Henry Kramer, inquisitors for the Catholic Church, wrote the *Malleus Maleficarum* as a handbook for dealing with witches and witchcraft. It was the first book of its kind. Some contend the Catholic church banned it; however, it was published thirteen times between 1487 and 1520 and sixteen times between 1574 to 1669. *Malleus Maleficarum* became the official standard by which inquisitors identified and persecuted witches. Between 1500 and 1660, the Inquisition killed up to eighty thousand people suspected of witchcraft in Europe; many estimate the number to be far greater. Wicasta Lovelace, who wrote the introduction to the 1948 edition of *Malleus Maleficarum*, attributed these deaths to the power of shared community systems of belief.

> It must be remembered that the Malleus is a work of its time. Science had only just begun to make any real advances. At that time nearly any unexplainable illness or malady would often be attributed to magic, and thus the activity of witches. It was a way for ordinary people to make sense of the world around them. The Malleus drew upon those beliefs, and, by its very existence, reinforced them and brought them into the codified belief system of the Catholic Church. In many ways, it could be said that it helped to validate the Inquisition itself.

The Quaker and Puritan Migration

During the English Civil War (1642–1651), Puritans (English protestants) sought to reform the Church of England by purging many Roman Catholic practices. The Puritans aligned themselves with parliamentary opposition and ousted King Charles I. Their victory gained them a foothold from which they could rise to power within the church and government.

Out of the English Civil War came several other radical, nonconformist Christian groups like the Quakers. They believed God could speak to average people through his risen son outside of church authority. They abhorred corrupt and deceitful practices within the church, officially embraced pacifism, and offered equality to women within the church.

While they shared some similar beliefs about open worship with the Quakers, the Puritans despised them for their liberal attitudes, which challenged the social and political order. As the Quaker movement gained steam in the early 1650s, Oliver Cromwell, England's leader at the time and himself a Puritan, sided with the Puritans. He authorized the arrest of many Quakers and jailed them for their extremist beliefs, which some labeled the "work of the devil." In 1660, when the monarchy returned to power, much of the government and church structure returned to pre–Civil War status, and the Crown ejected thousands of Puritan ministers from the Church of England.

Formal persecution of Quakers continued in 1662, however, with the Quaker Act. This law required all Quakers to swear an oath of allegiance to the king, but religious conviction prevented them from doing so. Two years later, the Conventicle Act of 1664 targeted all non-conformist protestants by forbidding unauthorized church meetings of more than five people outside a single family. This oppression led to the Quaker and Puritan migration to America.

In 1620, a group of church dissenters who were a little too "pure" for even their Protestant counterparts left England and lived in the Netherlands for several years before a variety of circumstances pushed them to travel on to America. After a long journey across the Atlantic, the group settled near an abandoned Wampanoag village in an area Captain John Smith had previously named Plymouth. Because this group traveled in pursuit of religious freedom and were the first settlers of the Massachusetts colonies, they eventually became known as the Pilgrims.

By this time, a Patuxet Indian named Squanto, who had grown up in a village in what was now Plymouth, had already been sold into slavery, rescued by Spanish friars, and employed by a colonist named John Slaney, who arranged for Squanto to work as a guide. Squanto eventually returned to his village to find his people had perished from disease. The next year, more English colonists arrived. Instead of joining a different tribe, Squanto stayed with the new arrivals to help them survive the brutal winter. In the spring, he taught them how to work the land.

Non-dissenting Puritans also began trekking to North America in the 1630s. For some, it was to seek a better life, but for most the goal was to help establish English colonies in Massachusetts. The earliest settlements were the Massachusetts Bay Colony, the Saybrook Colony, the Connecticut Colony, and the New Haven Colony. These folks still wanted to be part of the Church of England, and many returned to England after they established the settlements. Many also stayed, and this territory became heavily influenced by the Puritan way of life. Church and government were still very much intertwined, but not with everyone's approval.

In 1636, the Massachusetts Bay colony banished a man named Roger Williams because he advocated for religious tolerance and the separation of church and state. Williams went on to found the state of Rhode Island along with Anne Hutchinson. Rhode Island became an early haven for those who opposed the rigidity of Puritanical control.

FUN FACT: Anne Hutchinson, spiritual leader to both men and women, became America's first feminist. She is credited as the only woman in history who helped found one of the original thirteen colonies.

In 1634, forty-three-year-old Anne Hutchinson, her husband, and their twelve children emigrated to Massachusetts from England. She began teaching salvation of grace from the Bible and soon developed a significant following of men and women. Her teachings opposed the Puritans' Covenant of Works and their belief that women should hold no positions of authority. Anne was arrested and jailed for what the Massachusetts Bay Colony leaders said were heretical beliefs. While in jail, the pregnant Anne lost her baby, as did her friend and fellow midwife, Mary Dyer, whose baby was born severely deformed. Leaders of the colony labeled their suffering the judgment of God. They accused Anne of being an instrument of the devil and banished her from the Massachusetts colony in 1637.

The Hutchinsons and Dyers, along with many other families, moved to Rhode Island where Anne became active in governmental affairs and biblical teaching. Mary Dyer converted to Quakerism and returned to Boston, where she was eventually executed, as it was unlawful for Quakers to live in Boston.

The Witch Trials

In the mid-1600s in Europe and America, nearly everyone experienced disease epidemics, war, political strife, and loss. There were no medicinal or scientific explanations and few effective remedies. There was no one to blame except the devil, and what could they do to counteract his evil schemes? Blame offers instant gratification only when there is an object to receive that blame. So men of power reinterpreted the Bible and defined witchcraft in a way that provided easy access to innocent scapegoats. They'd found a way to attack Satan, and it was a way that justified acting on emotion instead of applying thought and reason.

The first American "witch trial" took place in Windsor, Connecticut in 1647. The court found Alse Young and at least five other women guilty and hanged them. The first actual "witch hunt" took place in Hartford, Connecticut, in 1662, after eight-year-old Elizabeth Kelly came home from time spent with their neighbor, Goodwife Ayres. The girl fell ill and made accusations that Goody Ayres was hurting her. When Elizabeth died, the parents accused Goody of witchcraft. Not long after this, Ann Cole became ill and taken with "strange fits." She accused Rebecca Greensmith, a neighbor not well-liked by many because of her "lewd and ignorant ways."

Greensmith admitted her guilt and accused her husband and seven others of meeting with her in the woods. Her guilt was apparent when she and her husband failed the water test as outlined in the *Malleus Maleficarum*. The water test comprised stripping off the clothing of the accused, binding their hands and feet, and tossing them into the nearest body of water. According to the guidelines, a witch would float. Rebecca and her husband both surfaced and were therefore considered guilty of conniving with the devil. In all, forty-six prosecutions and eleven executions took place.

Thirty years later, money and politics were still at the center of conflict as refugees fleeing King William's War from the north flooded the Village of Salem in the Massachusetts Bay Colony. The population overwhelmed resources. Rivalries between wealthy families erupted. On top of this, Salem Village's first ordained minister, Samuel Parris, had revealed himself to be greedy and cruel. In this atmosphere of political division, commercial rivalries, and religious dissent, witchcraft accusations became a ready means of seeking revenge and discrediting rivals.

When Samuel Parris's nine-year-old daughter and eleven-year-old niece began having fits, a local doctor blamed the devil (or rather a witch).

Eleven-year-old Ann Putnam experienced similar symptoms. During questioning, the three girls were pressured into naming "the witches" responsible for their affliction. From here, the hunt began. Accusations were made, followed by fear and paranoia, which brought more accusations.

In charge at the time was Massachusetts's newly appointed governor William Phips, whose top priority was negotiating Native American conflicts. Because transferring the governorship had created a backlog of witch trials, Phips set up a court of oyer and terminer to hear and determine truth, a method typically used for petty crimes. He handed the court over to lieutenant governor William Stoughton and left to tackle matters with the Native Americans. Stoughton plowed through the trials, allowing spectral evidence (dreams and visions) and the use of torture. In just four months, he'd authorized the death of twenty people.

When Phips returned and found his own wife accused, he put a stop to the witch-trial madness, ended the court of oyer, and freed many of the prisoners. He publicly apologized for his part in the atrocity. Stoughton did not.

Powerful men and women were forging a new life in America with conflicting ideas about church and state. Church control of the government wasn't working. William Penn knew it, so colonies like Pennsylvania and New Jersey—under Quaker influence—muddled along with loosely structured and slightly chaotic governments. Quakers would not resort to violence or banish people from the colony, but they clung to their beliefs.

At the beginning of the Age of Enlightenment, scientific discoveries were joining the scholarly tradition of astrology as a means of understanding the unknown, and the Quakers felt threatened, afraid science and mysticism would shift and corrupt the worldview of their community. This was the atmosphere in which Daniel Leeds found himself as he attempted to explain his embrace of new ideas in *The Temple of Wisdom for the Little World, in Two Parts*. The book had been his grand attempt to show his neighbors how Quaker lifestyle could be improved by entertaining new scientific findings. But fear of witchcraft still hung in the air and Daniel's shifting worldview placed him apart from the Quaker community. Offended and hurt, Daniel retaliated, and the ensuing conflict gave rise to a monster. The Leeds Devil became the scapegoat needed for the misfortunes of those who had no one else to blame.

Mothman

A Legend Shrouded in Secrets

The Iroquoian-speaking Seneca called the waters bordering the southern region of their territory, *Ohiyo*, meaning, "beautiful river." What we call the Ohio River begins at the confluence of the Allegheny and Monongahela Rivers near Pittsburgh and flows 981 miles west to Cairo, Illinois, where it feeds into the Mississippi River. Over 25 million people live in the Ohio River Basin, one of the most populated and industrialized regions in the United States.

Small towns like Point Pleasant depended heavily on industry, river traffic, and a lifestyle centered around hard work, family, and simple living. But while the river brought prosperity and opportunity, it also brought destruction and hardship. This has been the ebb and flow of Point Pleasant's existence.

It was speculated that French explorer Robert Cavelier de La Salle was the first European to see the area around Point Pleasant during his voyage into the Ohio valley in 1669, but the proof of French claim to the land was found in 1805 when a couple of boys discovered a lead plate buried at the mouth of the Kanawha River by Captain Cléron de Bienville, who'd made the voyage in 1749.

Finding it sooner wouldn't have stopped the British from settling the land. When George Washington traveled down the Ohio River in 1770, he thought the area where the Kanawha River flows into the Ohio so appealing he named it Point Pleasant and desired to make this location a capital of its own colony. While that idea never materialized, royal governor John Murray, also known as Lord Dunmore, gave instructions to build Fort Blair at the confluence to aid in the expansion of British territory.

After the Battle of Point Pleasant in 1774—what some deem the first battle of the American Revolution—Native Americans burned the Fort. The next year, a company of men traveled down the river from Fort Pitt and rebuilt the structure under the command of Captain Matthew Arbuckle. They called the new garrison Fort Randolph, and it became an important fortification, offering back door support to the colonists during the revolution.

In 1794, the General Assembly of Virginia gave two hundred acres of land to form the community of Point Pleasant. One early resident, Daniel Boone, helped carve Mason County out of Kanawha County, making Point

Pleasant the county seat. The town was incorporated in 1833, but growth was slow until shipyards began to appear in the 1840s. The first census, taken in 1879, recorded approximately 770 people. After the great flood of 1913, rebuilding included the incorporation of new industry to support the growing use of river transportation, an important factor in making Point Pleasant a boomtown.

The Age of Industry

On the Ohio side of the river, the Marietta Manufacturing Company was hit hard by the great flood and lost its president as well. In 1914, Walter Augustus Windsor was only twenty-three years old when he inherited the presidency of the nearly dead company. Leaving his family and moving the factory to Point Pleasant, West Virginia, was not an easy decision, but Windsor enlisted the help of C. O. Weissenburger and other industry professionals who agreed the move was a good idea.

In 1916, the new team opened operations in West Virgina at the foot of Twenty-Second Street, in what locals call the heights district. They hoped the elevation of the facilities would offer protection in the event of another catastrophic flood. Less than a year after opening, the company secured contracts to make boilers and engines for the military during World War I. They expanded operations in 1918 to include full-scale ship building and then won a contract with the U.S. Railroad to build four towboats.

After Walter Windsor died in 1929, C. O. Weissenburger took over as president. Between 1930 and 1965, the company built ninety-four ships for the military, seventy-three of which were first used in World War II. The largest of these ships were Army mine planters that measured 188 feet in length and 37 feet wide. The Marietta Manufacturing Company thrived, employing upwards of three thousand people at its peak of operation. But this fortune did not last. Due to economic decline in the 60s, the company ceased operation in 1970. Amherst Industries bought the facilities and op-

---

FUN FACT: To get large, oceangoing ships down the Ohio River, the Marietta Manufacturing Company would have the Army Corps of Engineers open the gates at Racine Dam (238 miles downstream from Pittsburgh). The released water would push the ship to the next dam, where they would repeat the operation. Ships rode the waves from one dam to the next, all the way to the Mississippi River.

Mine Planter built at the Marietta Manufacturing Company in Point Pleasant, WV. Mines were dropped over the side or behind the ship at pre-defined intervals. Photo credit: Marietta Manufacturing Company Records (#742), Special Collections Department, J. Y. Joyner Library, East Carolina University, Greenville, North Carolina, U.S.A.

erated under the name Point Pleasant Marine, offering boat repairs and equipment until 1984, when a strike forced their shutdown.

In 1942, approximately six miles north of Point Pleasant, the United States Army built and operated the West Virginia Ordinance Works on 8,323 acres of land. The sole purpose of the facility was to produce 720,000 tons of TNT per day for the war effort. The complete site included power plants, acid storage and concentration facilities, rail yards and river dock sites, administrative offices, housing, repair shops, and magazine storage units. Laborers were in high demand, so local men working at the plant were exempt from military service.

On August 15, 1945, victory over Japan ceased all TNT manufacturing operations at the ordinance works. Cleanup and distribution of surplus materials began in accordance with Department of War instructions. According to a history of the Point Pleasant facility by the nonprofit think tank GlobalSecurity.org, "By November 1949 all the plumbing and process equipment associated with the TNT manufacturing area had been removed except for the contaminated sewer lines running to the Red and Yellow Water Lines. The sewers were blocked off and abandoned in place, as they were not considered a hazard." The government sold some of the land to private parties who dealt in explosives—a perfect solution since the ammunition magazines, or concrete bungalows, remained intact. Mason Furniture Company operated on part of the property from 1948 to 1970. Other buildings stood empty.[1]

Age of Suspicion

The nuclear age exploded onto the scene July 16, 1945, when the United States tested the Trinity bomb in the New Mexico desert. The tennis-ball sized plutonium sphere was equivalent to twenty thousand tons of TNT. A month later, when two nuclear bombs killed eighty thousand people in Japan, effectively ending World War II, the devastating effects of atomic weaponry impacted the hearts and minds of everyone on the planet.

While physical conflict ceased, an intangible conflict continued between the capitalist ideals of the United States and the communist ideals of the USSR. Out of this power struggle emerged a nuclear arms and space race fraught with paranoia and fear that the other side would become the stronger. In a famous essay for the *Tribune*, George Orwell dubbed this era of global tension and nuclear anxiety the "Cold War," observing that this period in time was "a peace that is no peace."[2]

Mao and communism had taken over China in 1949, the same year the Soviet Union detonated their first atomic bomb. As fears of global nuclear war escalated and several high-profile cases of espionage came to light, Wisconsin senator Joseph McCarthy went on a national witch hunt to expose communist sympathizers he believed were hiding among the American public. Most of the accused were left-wing Americans with strong political beliefs—union workers, authors, Hollywood artists, and government officials. Included on the FBI watch list were Helen Keller, Burl Ives, Orson Welles, and Martin Luther King Jr.

As television became a middle-class mainstay, Americans took a front-row seat and watched as Senator McCarthy escalated to publicly attacking the armed services. Because of his bullying tactics and false accusations, the senator lost credibility and power. But his fear-mongering tactics had affected the American mindset. Many believed spies and traitors riddled the government. American leadership could not be trusted. The world could not be trusted.

Television served another purpose for the American public. With the world twisting into a knot of Red Scare tension, most TV-watching Americans preferred to come home from work and escape. By the mid-1950s half of all US homes owned a television and tuned in to watch the most popular sitcom of the day, "Leave it to Beaver," which aired on CBS/ABC from 1957 to 1963. The show premiered the day the Soviet Union announced the launch of Sputnik I and aired its final episode two months before the assassination of president John F. Kennedy. In between, the world witnessed the space race, the threat of nuclear war, the Soviet Union's determination to undermine the United States, and the Cuban Missile Crisis.

Talk of flying saucers and government conspiracies entered the mainstream media after the first widely reported UFO sighting in 1947, near Mount Rainier in Washington State. Pilot Kenneth Arnold was searching for a downed plane when he saw several crescent-shaped objects that moved so fast they looked "like a saucer if you skip it across the water." A reporting newspaper mistakenly said they were "saucer-shaped," coining the term "flying saucers."[3]

Sightings of unidentified aerial phenomena increased, and in 1948 the U.S. Air Force created Project Sign to investigate UFO sightings. Headquartered at Wright-Patterson Air Force Base in Dayton, Ohio, Project Sign (1947–49) was soon replaced by Project Grudge (1949–52). Project Blue Book replaced Project Grudge. From 1952 to 1969 Project Blue Book compiled over twelve thousand reports, classifying them as either "identified"— meaning they were attributable to a known astronomical, atmospheric, or artificial (manmade) phenomenon—or "unidentified."

As the number of sightings continued to grow, the CIA put together an expert panel of scientists led by Howard P. Robertson. This group reviewed the Project Blue Book cases and determined that ninety percent of them could be explained by natural phenomena or earthly objects. They found no evidence for the ETH (extraterrestrial hypothesis), nor was there any evident threat to national security. But the government kept these findings a secret until 1979, launching a nationwide flying-saucer frenzy.

FUN FACT: J. Allen Hynek, an astronomer involved with Projects Sign, Grudge, and Blue Book said that a few of the most-reliable UFO reports offered definitive indications of extraterrestrial visitors. Hynek went on to found the Center for UFO Studies (CUFOS), which continues to investigate sightings today.

The first mysterious Man in Black appeared in June 1947. Harold Dahl, a conservationist, said he witnessed six donut-shaped vessels floating over Puget Sound where he and his dog sat in a boat. One of the hovering vessels fell, killing his dog. Dahl took pictures with his camera and showed his supervisor, Fred Crisman. The following day, Dahl said a man in a black suit visited him and warned him to remain silent. Dahl and Crisman later admitted the incident was a hoax, but the story went on to be published in Gray Barker's book, *They Knew Too Much about Flying Saucers* (1956).

Also included in the book was a story told by World War II veteran Albert Bender. A UFO enthusiast, Bender founded the International Flying Saucer Bureau and became deeply involved in research on UFOs and mental telepathy. Bender said that in 1953, three men dressed in black visited his Bridgeport, Connecticut, home and warned him to stop researching and publishing in the magazine *Space Review*. The CIA, shrouded in secrecy, had not released any findings from Project Blue Book, and stories like those in Gray Barker's book sparked interest.

By the early 1950s, the United States government felt an urgent need to spy on the Soviet Union and China, but military aircraft could not make shallow-penetration flights into remote areas without great risk. This led to the development of the U-2, a high-performance surveillance aircraft, in 1954. To avoid Cold War escalation in the event of capture, top secret U-2 surveillance missions were never flown by American military pilots. Instead, civilians and pilots who had resigned their commissions flew the U-2, and, with the greatest secrecy, infiltrated deep into the Soviet Union and parts of Asia. But where and how did they test these planes without discovery? Were test flights actually observed by Americans and passed off as UFO sightings? Secret keeping often feels like lying, so it's no wonder UFO sightings escalated in the 1950s and '60s or that Americans became skeptical of their own government.

It was during this flurry of UFO activity that Mothman and the Men in Black arrived in Point Pleasant, West Virginia. Is it possible the Mothman sightings in 1966 and 1967 were an elaborately arranged cover up? Was there some covert operation taking place that required a diversion? Something with Vietnam? Or new classified equipment being tested over the remote regions of West Virginia? As U-2 pilots were captured and evidence of secret government programs came to light, suspicions grew about what else the US government was up to.

It wouldn't be the first time cryptids and government operations mixed. There is long-standing speculation that 1940 and 1950 expeditions into Nepal in search of the Yeti were a cover for CIA operations. Ivan T. Sanderson, a famed cryptozoologist, was a commander with the British Naval Intelligence Service. One of his close friends, W. M. Russell, an American who had attended school at Cambridge, also served in the British Navy. Russell found his way into China by assisting Ruth Harkness in the capture of the first live giant panda. He returned to China in the late 1940s to try to capture an animal called the golden takin but was forced to leave by the communist army. Soon after, both Russell and Sanderson joined an expedition into Tibet in search of the Yeti led by a businessman and cryptid enthusiast named Tom Slick.

Slick was a millionaire from Houston whose family fortune was seeded in the oil and railroad businesses. He expressed a deep interest in cryptids while in college and traveled the world to investigate their existence. Prior to the Yeti expeditions in 1958 and 1959, he and his brother operated an air-cargo company linked to the CIA in Asia.

All over the planet, famous figures in the world of cryptozoology penetrated remote regions in search of the unknown. Or was it to spy? Some people think the government was hiding activity within or around the TNT plant north of Point Pleasant, West Virginia. Whether Mothman was extraterrestrial or earthly, no one can say, but the many unusual sightings of the flying cryptid, reports of visits from Men in Black, and unusual lights in the night sky fueled conspiracy theories and popular interest in cryptids. Thousands of people flocked to Point Pleasant to glimpse Mothman—or to catch Mothman if they could.

The Silver Bridge collapse, the escalating conflict in Vietnam, and the close of the Marietta Manufacturing Company all happened about the same time. Did these events, combined with the tension and paranoia of the Cold War and nuclear age, offer a perfect storm of anxieties that encouraged the mind to play tricks? Folks living in and around Point Pleasant were dealing with serious issues that impacted their quality of life. For many, especially the conspiracy minded, their landscape and their worldviews were changing.

FUNFACT: The central Intelligence Agency came into existence in 1947 to provide intelligence in matters of national security to the president and senior policymakers. No one knows how many people work for the CIA.

Age of the Curse

Many still say the events that took place at Point Pleasant between November 1966 and December 1967 resulted from a curse enacted upon the land by Shawnee Chief Cornstalk. For a town of its size in a remote location, Point Pleasant does seem to have been hit hard over the years. Despite solid evidence against the theory that Chief Cornstalk had cursed the community, people believed in the curse, or needed to believe in it. Otherwise, how could so many bad things happen to one community without cause? Blame is a powerful release in hard times, even though it rarely leads to a solution.

When invoking Cornstalk's curse, many people reference the tragedies we've listed on the following timeline, and we sympathize with the friends and family of those who experienced loss due to these tragedies. But horrific events and natural disasters happen around the world, and one has to wonder if the string of tragic events in and near Point Pleasant aren't coincidental.

We placed the mileage after some accidents to address the question, What are the boundaries of a curse? How far does one have to go to escape its grasp?

1907   Three hundred and sixty-two miners die in Monongah, West Virginia (144 miles from Point Pleasant)

1913   Entire town of Point Pleasant floods, leading to 650 deaths along the Ohio River

1937   Entire town of Point Pleasant floods, leading to 350 deaths along the Ohio River

1944   The most deadly tornado to hit West Virginia kills 104 people. The hardest hit area was Shinnston, West Virginia, in Harrison County (136 miles from Point Pleasant).

1967   The Silver Bridge connecting Point Pleasant, West Virginia, and Gallipolis, Ohio, collapses into the Ohio River, killing 46 people.

1968   A Piedmont Airlines plane runs into fog as it approaches Kanawha Airport in Charleston, West Virginia, and crashes, killing 35 people (56 miles from Point Pleasant).

1970   Southern Airways Flight 932, carrying 37 members of the Marshall University Thundering Herd football team, crashes into a hill just short of the Tri-State Airport, killing all 75 people on board (52 miles from Point Pleasant)

1978   A freight train derailment contaminates the town of Point Pleasant's water supply

1978   Scaffolding inside the cooling tower of an unfinished power plant at Willow Island, West Virginia, owned by the Monongahela Power Company tears loose, and 51 workers fall 170 feet to their deaths (73 miles from Point Pleasant)

1981   Red water seepage is found at the McClintic State Wildlife Management Area. Point Pleasant ground water is contaminated with TNT and hazardous by-products[4]

During times of crisis, grief can expand belief systems or change them. The actual power of a curse depends on the way a person (or community) bounces back after falling down.

The Haunt Factor

In the preface to his satirical novel *The Screwtape Letters* (1941) based on the correspondence between two demons, C. S. Lewis writes: "There are two equal and opposite errors into which our race can fall about the devils. One is to disbelieve in their existence. The other is to believe, and to feel an excessive and unhealthy interest in them."

According to the Bible, when Lucifer (Satan) rebelled against God, he fell from Heaven to earth. Many other angels followed. This legion of demons continues to roam the earth with a single goal—to divide man from God. In his book *The Invisible World* (2011), Anthony DeStefano writes that humans have a spiritual component—the soul—that allows for built in "haunt detectors": "Everybody has one. . . . It's the little alarm that goes off in our heads whenever we detect that something mysterious or supernatural has occurred. You could be sitting around relaxing one day at home, and for no special reason you start thinking about someone. Maybe you haven't thought about this person in years. Then the phone rings; you pick it up, and amazingly, it's that person! Many of us have experienced this phenomenon."[5]

In *The Mothman Prophecies* (1975), John Keel writes about a lone visit he made to the TNT plant at night. While he wasn't afraid for most of the visit —even during his time spent inside the abandoned building—there was one stretch of road that caused him to feel significant fear. He purposely drove through the area a second time, sensing the same dreadful feeling. After parking his car along the side of the road, he slowly walked toward the area and noted the exact step where his emotions shifted. He could see nothing with his eyes, but he sensed evil. Those who encountered Mothman and the Men in Black often describe an uneasy feeling accompanied by unreasonable fear.

Is Mothman a demon? A spiritual entity that tormented a community? Did he induce a "haunt factor" or cause or foretell the collapse of the Silver Bridge? No one can be certain about the nature or purpose of the cryptid's appearance, but we know that a crack in eyebar number 330 is what caused the bridge to collapse. Were demons somehow responsible for that crack? Or were demons simply hanging about the area, waiting for the tragedy to occur so they could bask in the human misery like pigs in mud?

We live in an age where information exists at our fingertips. The menagerie of beliefs can feel like a circus, but what we believe and who we listen to are significant. These are the factors that influence the way we interpret our world. Logic. Religion. Secrets and conspiracies. Curses. Angels and Demons. Throughout the ages, these have all been instrumental forces shaping our beliefs surrounding flying cryptids and unknown entities. How about you? What is your belief system surrounding these sky monsters?

Sky Monsters in Pop Culture

A captivation with flight has always pulled at the human need to explore and fed a desire for adventure. But that pull does not stop with airplanes and helicopters. The natural ability of birds to skillfully perform amazing feats in the air adds to the fascination people have with our endless overhead expanse.

Exploring the unknown through the world of cryptids allows a person to test the limits of imagination and creativity. While not every encounter with sky monsters in pop culture centers on flight, risk and adventure are common threads. We'll open this section with one of the greatest risk-takers of all times.

Fantastic Fliers

1927—CHARLES LINDBERGH AND THE BRIDGE OF THE GODS

Charles Lindbergh became a national hero and gained worldwide fame after completing the first nonstop solo trans-Atlantic flight in May 1927. Later that year, in September, he was asked to help celebrate the opening of a new bridge erected over the Columbia River in Cascade Locks, Oregon. The cantilever bridge was made from eighty thousand pounds of steel that stretched 1,858 feet at full-length and stood 91 feet over the water.

A legendary flier, Colonel Lindbergh was the perfect celebrity to help dedicate a landmark that referenced another legend of the skies. The original Bridge of the Gods land bridge was thought to have been caused by landslides about one thousand years ago. Native America tribes tell a couple of different stories of how the land bridge came to be; the most widely known states the "great spirit" buried Thunderbird under crumbling rock. His massive body and outstretched wings allowed the people to cross over the great river. You can read more on this legend in chapter 3 of this book: "History and Legends."

Charles Lindbergh was born February 4, 1902, in Detroit, but he grew up on a farm in Minnesota. He attended the University of Wisconsin to study engineering but left after two years to become a barnstormer, performing aerial stunts in planes. In 1924, he enlisted in the army to become a pilot in the Army Air Service Reserve. After graduating top of his class from the U.S. Army's flight school, he took a job flying mail from Chicago to St. Louis.

In 1925, Lindbergh entered the 1911 Raymond Orteig competition to fly the first solo nonstop from New York City to Paris, France. The winning prize was $25,000. Several men had entered and died, but Lindbergh was confident he could make it with the right plane—and he did. After receiving financial backing from two St. Louis businessmen, Lindbergh worked with an aeronautical company out of San Diego to manufacture a special airplane for the trans-Atlantic flight. He named his winning plane *The Spirit of St. Louis*.

Of his life in the air, Lindberg said, "The life of an aviator seemed to me ideal. It involved skill. It brought adventure. It made use of the latest developments of science. Mechanical engineers were fettered to factories and drafting boards while pilots have the freedom of wind with the expanse of sky. There were times in an aeroplane when it seemed I had escaped mortality to look down on earth like a God."[6]

On September 1927, Lindbergh flew *The Spirit of St. Louis* on another famous flight, this time up the Columbia River gorge from Portland, Oregon, to dedicate the Bridge of the Gods between Washington State and Oregon. Having left the two-year-old Swan Island Airport surrounded by an eager crowd of onlookers, Lindbergh passed low over the new bridge, offering the crowd a decent view. Downriver, he banked his plane and, in a dramatic show of barnstorming talent, made a sharp and clean 180 degree turn before flying back under the bridge and back to Portland.

©2019 Mel Cabre

1939—THE 45TH INFANTRY DIVISION,
AKA THE THUNDERBIRD DIVISION

Embedded in American history and pride are the characteristics of the Native American warrior. Nowhere is this more clear than in the United States military, where men and women sacrifice their lives to protect their land and people.

FUN FACT: Many U.S. military helicopters have been named for Native American tribes. Those currently in service are the Lakota, the Blackhawk, the Apache, the Chinook, the Kiowa, the Cayuse, the Creek, and the Ute.

The 45th Infantry Division, active from 1920 to 1968, was part of the Oklahoma Army National Guard and Infantry Division of the United States Army. Headquartered mostly in Oklahoma City, the guardsmen fought in both World War II and the Korean War. The division's original shoulder sleeve insignia featured a swastika, at the time a peaceful Native American symbol showing pride and unity. This symbol paid tribute to the large representation of Native Americans from the Southwestern United States that served in the 45th Infantry.

With the rise of the Nazi party and the symbol's association with prejudice and hatred, the 45th Division stopped using the insignia and underwent a long process of getting a new one. In 1939, a design by Woody Big Bow, a Kiowa artist from Carnegie, Oklahoma, was chosen as a replacement. It featured a golden Thunderbird on a red square. The red and gold paid tribute to the Spanish settlers of the four major states represented in the division: Arizona, Colorado, New Mexico, and Oklahoma.

The 45th Infantry Division became one of the most decorated units in World War II, with nine Medal of Honor recipients. They also received sixty-one Distinguished Service Crosses, three Distinguished Service Medals, 1,848 Silver Star Medals, thirty-eight Legion of Merit medals, fifty-nine Soldier's Medals, 5,744 Bronze Star Medals, and 52 Air Medals. The division received seven distinguished unit citations and eight campaign streamers during the conflict.[7]

1953—THUNDERBIRD AIR COMBAT COMMAND UNIT

The Thunderbirds are a United States Air Force Air Combat Command unit that performs precision maneuvers to show off the aerial capabilities of the pilots and the latest in fighter-jet technology. The unit currently operates the F-16 Fighting Falcon. In the past they have flown the F-84G Thunderjet, the F-100 Super Sabre, the F-105 Thunderchief, the F4E-Phantom, and the T-38 Talon.

The F-16 is a highly maneuverable, multi-role fighter plane proven to be one of the world's best aircraft, both as a tactical bomber and for use in air-to-air combat. To prepare them for air shows, the only needed modifications are replacing the 20mm cannon with a smoke-generating system and, of course, painting the planes with the Thunderbird unit colors and design.[8]

Created in 1953, the USAF Thunderbirds are one of the oldest formal flying aerobatic teams in the world. Designated the 3600th Air Demonstration Unit, the Thunderbirds were first activated at Luke Air Force Base, Arizona. They called themselves the Thunderbirds because of the strong Native American culture in the southwestern United States where Luke Air Force Base was located. Today, the Thunderbird squadron is assigned to the 57th Wing and is based at Nellis Air Force Base in Nevada.

Photo by wyldwest (https://www.flickr.com/photos/22047513@N00) is licensed under CC by SA 2.0.

1956—THE ORIGINAL THUNDERBIRD STEAKHOUSE AND CATERING

Located in Broomall, Pennsylvania, the family-owned Thunderbird restaurant serves award-winning cheesesteaks, hoagies, pizzas, and wings. They also offer breakfast, daily specials, and online ordering. While the restaurant might have been named after the car, the restaurant's logo is a bright and colorful giant bird.[9]

The Philadelphia Inquirer writes, "As the Eagles fly, so does Thunderbird, the Delco steak shop that is all fight and heart." At this writing they had just celebrated sixty-three years. Their website states, "Thunderbird has become a regular stop to eat and unwind, a place where friends come to dine and share stories in what has now become a timeless place. Stop by, settle into a classic wooden booth, and enjoy a meal in a dining area covered with pictures of yester-year. Enjoy an old fashion milkshake and the area's best cheesesteak."[10]

1971—THE SEATTLE THUNDERBIRDS: #ITSTARTSNOW

A major Western Hockey League junior ice hockey team, the Seattle Thunderbirds have been a leading source of talented players for the National Hockey League for over forty years. The teams' home rink, the ShoWare Center, is located eighteen miles south of downtown Seattle in the city of Kent. The WHL is a member of the Canadian Hockey League and comprises twenty-two member clubs—seventeen in Canada and five in the U.S. Pacific Northwest.

Education is important to the Thunderbirds. All players must attend school at Kentwood High School. Once students graduate, the team encourages them to attend a local college, the University of Washington, or a different college of their choice. For every season a player plays in the WHL, they receive a guaranteed full-year scholarship to a post-secondary institution, which includes tuition, textbooks, and compulsory fees. Further demonstrating their philanthropic nature, every year the WHL and its member clubs contribute over one million dollars to support Junior Hockey and other charities.

The Thunderbirds started out in 1971 as the Vancouver Nats. After a few moves and changes, they settled in Seattle and were named the Thunderbirds by their new owner. The team's logo depicts a Native American carving of a thunderbird with the word "Seattle" etched into it, framed by two hockey sticks. Cool Bird the Thunderbird is the official representative of the Seattle Thunderbirds. He appears at games and local events to help promote the team.[11]

2015—JURASSIC WORLD

Starring Chris Pratt and Bryce Dallas Howard.
Rated PG-13 for violence and gore.
Set in Central America, but filmed on the islands of Kauai and Oahu,
    Hawaii.

Control is a key word in this movie. "It's always about control with you. . . . You are not in control here," says Claire (Bryce Dallas Howard) as she desperately tries to maintain control while a giant genetically modified dinomaniac is on the loose.

If you've seen this movie, then you'll no doubt remember the famous scene where the mega-sized *Mosasaurus* propels himself out of the water Shamu-style to swallow an entire great white shark. He drops back into the depths of the tank, drenching the audience. A well-designed scene crafted to foreshadow his amazing jumping abilities.

©2019 Mel Cabre.

The birdcage within Jurassic World houses a variety of pterosaurs, including the *Dimorphodon*, which some cryptozoologists believe bears a close resemblance to the Ropen (more about the Ropen in chapter 5). When the powerful, crafty, and genetically modified *Indominus rex* plows through the cage, destroying it, the fliers break free. One runs his pointed beak through the windshield of a helicopter, spearing a man. The helicopter crashes. As the flying reptiles descend on the crowded theme park, the attendees take off running. A large *Pteranodon* snatches a running woman in its talons but drops her as he flies out over the water. He dives in, recapturing her in his oversized beak, but just as he emerges from the water, feast in mouth, the *Mosasaurus* surges out of the water and eats them both.

This monster movie grossed over a billion dollars worldwide and proved how much people love dinosaurs . . . and monsters.

2016—FANTASTIC BEASTS AND WHERE TO FIND THEM

"From J. K. Rowling's Wizarding World."
Written by J. K. Rowling.
Adventure, Fantasy.
Rated PG-13 for moderate violence, gore, frightening scenes, mild profanity,
*   smoking, and use of alcohol.*
With a budget of $180 million, the movie grossed $814 million worldwide.

Full of drama and intrigue, this movie takes place in 1926 New York and is part of the action-packed Harry Potter universe. The protagonist, Newt Scamander, makes up the excuse he needs to travel to America—he says he needs to buy a magical creature for a birthday present. His real goal is to return the Thunderbird he saved from being trafficked in Egypt back to the wilds of Arizona. Unfortunately, a succession of events at the outset of the movie force Newt into a mystery of major proportions, keeping him from his initial goal.

We first see the Thunderbird after Newt encourages his friend Jacob to join him in his suitcase of magical creatures, so he can heal the bite wound Jacob received when the murtlap escaped. As Jacob helps Newt feed the creatures, a giant Thunderbird soars overhead in a rain cloud emitting thunder and lightning.

The entire movie passes before we see the Thunderbird again: first, when the creature announces the upcoming climactic danger, and second, when he comes to save the day. Enlisting the Thunderbird's help means

Newt won't be able to return him to Arizona, but it's a small price to pay to keep the world of magic safe from "the most vicious creatures on earth . . . humans." The Thunderbird ascends into the sky carrying a potion that will erase memories and causes it to rain down on everyone and everything.

Distinguished Devils

1974—NEW JERSEY DEVILS HOCKEY

The New Jersey Devils are a professional ice hockey team based in Newark, New Jersey. The club was founded as the Kansas City Scouts in Kansas City, Missouri, in 1974. After a couple of moves, they settled in East Rutherford, New Jersey. In 2007, they moved to Newark where they currently play at the Prudential Center.

In 1982, over ten thousand people voted in a contest called, "Name That Team." The popular option appeared to be the New Jersey Devils, even though the potential name offended some: "One caller threatened the life of a New Jersey reporter who had written about the name contest, labeling him 'an agent of Satan.'" Despite the objections, The Jersey Devil name won by a large margin. The other options were the Americans, Blades, Colonials, Lightning, Meadowlarks, Meadowlanders, Coastals, Generals, Gulls, Jaguars, and Patriots.[12]

The Devils' logo is a monogrammed "N" and "J". Horns poke out of the J while the tail emerges from the N. The mascot is a seven-foot-tall devil, who replaced Slapshot, the horned hockey puck, in 1993. The New Jersey Devils franchise is the only major league team in any sport that explicitly identifies itself as a New Jersey team.

1981—THE HARDY BOYS SERIES #67

Published by Aladdin.
Written by Franklin W. Dixon, the pen name used by a variety of different
   authors who wrote the Hardy Boys novels.
190 pages.
Children's mystery, action, and adventure.

The Hardy Boys book #67, *The Outlaw's Silver*, takes place in the Pine Barrens of New Jersey. A mysterious letter from the Outlaw of the Pine Barrens, followed by a threatening letter from a dead man, draws Frank and Joe into a chilling adventure involving long-lost treasure, a gang of smugglers, and the Jersey Devil.

Edward Stratemeyer and his syndicate created the Hardy Boys in 1926, which then advertised for ghostwriters to write the stories from outlines the syndicate provided. The syndicate also created *Nancy Drew, Tom Swift,* and the *Rover Boys.* Since their release in 1927, the Hardy Boys have never gone out of print, and they remain popular today, with close to five hundred titles published across several series.

1997—*JERSEY DEVIL* (THE VIDEO GAME)

"The beast is loose. . . . Just try messing with him."
Behaviour Interactive.
Released for Play Station in 1997 and for PC in 1999.
Rating: E for Everyone.
Action, adventure, and comedy.

In a brightly animated opening, an adorable purple baby devil is brought to mad scientist Dr. Knarf by his pumpkin-headed sidekick, Dennis. In the lab, the doctor is experimenting on plants, changing them into evil mutants. As he is about to experiment on the new arrival, the devil wrecks the lab, blows it up, and escapes into Jersey City.

Many years pass. The evil doctor has resumed his efforts to terrorize the people of Jersey City with giant vegetable humanoids. But a grownup Jersey Devil, who has added red boots and gloves to his attire, has other plans. Eating pumpkins to maintain power, he watches over the city to defend and rescue its citizens, even though they are just as afraid of him as they are of the mutant vegetables.

2002—THE 13TH CHILD

"The Pine Barrens is a place full of secrets. . . . Those Who Believe Fear It.
Those Who Don't . . . Will."
The 2002 version stars Cliff Robertson, Michelle Maryk, and Robert
Guillaume.
Horror, thriller, mystery
Rated R for nudity, violence, and gore.
This movie was filmed inside the Pine Barrens at the Batsto Historic Site
located outside of Hammonton in the Wharton State Forest.

After a brief documentary-style opening and a flashback to a murder that takes place in the woods twenty years ago, the story begins in the present, on October 31. A paranormal show is playing on the TV in a mental health institution, recounting the origin of the Jersey Devil. The host explains the thirteenth child of a Leni Lenape shaman was hanged by British soldiers during the American Revolution because they feared his supernatural powers. As they were hanging him, the boy shape-shifted into a grotesque creature and killed the soldiers.

The TV show goes on to discuss the mutilation of an escaped convict that happened three days earlier. Mr. Riley, a mental health patient, breaks down after seeing the documentary. "Indians take scalps. The devil takes heads. Everyone is going to die," he says.

The local district attorney assigns her best cop, Kathryn (Michelle Maryk), to investigate the mutilation, hoping she can prove the Jersey Devil was responsible. Twenty years ago, her father went missing in the Pine Barrens while serving as a cop with Mr. Riley. She thinks it has something to do with the creature. Along with two other cops, Kathryn enters the Pine Barrens and learns more than she wanted to know about the legendary Jersey Devil.

2021—THE JERSEY DEVIL ROLLER COASTER

On August 29, 2019, Six Flags Great Adventure and Safari of Jackson, New Jersey, announced the upcoming "Jersey Devil Coaster" built by manufacturer Rocky Mountain Construction. Set to debut in 2021, the tallest, fastest, single-rail roller coaster in the United States begins with an 87-degree drop, twists and turns with a 180-degree stall, and moves into a zero-G roll that speeds into inline riders.

OTHER APPEARANCES

The Jersey Devil has made movie appearances in *Teenage Mutant Ninja Turtles* (2007) and *The Barrens* (2012). In TV series, his most famous appearance came October 8, 1993, in episode five of *The X-Files'* first season. Then, in 1995, the cryptid starred in *The Real Adventures of Johnny Quest*, season one, episode seventeen. In 2011, the Winchester brothers made a trip to the Pine Barrens to investigate unusual activity in season seven, episode nine of *Supernatural*.

The Jersey Devil also appears in two video games: *The Wolf Among Us* (2103), where he is an agent to the main villain, the Crooked Man, and *Poptropica* (2007) in which a player must search for the Jersey Devil and collect eggshells as proof of its existence.

Finally, the Jersey Devil was classically immortalized in a song by the legendary Bruce Springsteen who wrote "A Night with the Jersey Devil" to commemorate Halloween in 2008. It's a bluesy song about an eighteenth-century boy who grew hooves, a horse's head, bat wings, and a forked tail. Now, he haunts the Pine Barrens of south Jersey.

Mysterious Mothman

The first Mothman sighting took place in 1966 but the creature was formally introduced to the public in 1975 with the publication of John Keel's bestselling novel, *The Mothman Prophecies*. The cryptid catapulted to worldwide fame with the release of the 2002 major motion picture by the same name, starring Richard Gere.

The town of Point Pleasant capitalized on the attention by establishing the Mothman Museum. Attracting thousands of visitors each year, the museum features everything from original newspaper articles and handwritten testimonies to props from the movie and collectibles. A popular gift shop attached to the museum is devoted solely to Mothman and offers exclusive Mothman items. Besides hosting the store, the museum sponsors the annual Mothman Festival that brings in more than ten thousand fans a year, all of whom keep the Mothman legacy alive.

2002—MOTHMAN PROPHECIES: THE MOVIE

"What Do You See?"
Drama, horror, mystery, thriller.
Richard Gere.
Rated PG-13 for moderate violence, gore, and language.
The movie was successful, grossing over $55,000,000 worldwide.

While a small portion of this movie was made in Point Pleasant, West Virginia, most filming took place in Pennsylvania. Screenwriter Richard Hatem reworked Keel's book by creating a fictional protagonist, John Klein, who finds himself in Point Pleasant after his wife dies in a car crash. Before she dies, she draws images of a black flying creature that have continued to haunt Klein. He sets out on a trip to Virginia, but inexplicably finds himself in Point Pleasant, West Virginia, drawn into mysterious happenings he knows nothing about. As Klein learns others are seeing and experiencing visions of the creature who haunts him, he hunts for answers, sensing something brought him to Point Pleasant for a reason.

2017—THE MOTHMAN OF POINT PLEASANT

"13 Months That Changed History."
A Small Town Monsters Production.
Directed by Seth Breedlove.
Drama, horror, documentary.

The Small Town Monsters crew travels to Point Pleasant and interacts with locals who had encounters with Mothman in 1966 and 1967. Sharing history and local lore, this film offers a comprehensive look into the lives and times of a small community and what happened during those terrorizing thirteen months, including the collapse of the Silver Bridge. Great cinematography, animation, and stunning artwork add to the viewer experience.

A sequel by Small Town Monsters was released in 2020 called *The Mothman Legacy*. It follows even more frightening encounters while diving deep into the cryptid's legendary existence.

2018—FALLOUT 76

"Our Future Begins."
Action, adventure, mystery, science fiction.
Rated M for moderate violence, alcohol, drugs, smoking, and intense fighting.

Fallout 76 is a multi-player online game developed by Bethesda Game Studios and published by Bethesda Softworks. Released on Microsoft Windows, PlayStation 4, and Xbox One, *Fallout 76* is the newest installment in the Fallout series,

The game is set in post-apocalyptic Appalachia in an area known as the former state of West Virginia. The year is 2102. Twenty-five years after the Great War and before any previous *Fallout* games, players and their fellow vault mates emerge into the unknown world. To survive, players can journey alone or with others to explore, build, and triumph against monsters and other threats.

Occasionally, Mothman makes an appearance. He has become a favorite token for players to find and interact with.

2018 TO PRESENT—CRYPTKINS

"They Do Exist."
By Cryptozoic Entertainment.

These menacingly adorable vinyl cryptid characters are a little over two inches in height. Each series has thirteen different figures that come in their own mini crate. All boxes are a blind opening, so you don't know which figure you might get or whether any figures within a case might be duplicates. Each figurine comes with a bio card. A picture of the creature is on one side and information about the cryptid and the legend are on the other side.

Series one features Chupacabra, Cthulhu, Mothman, Nessie, Ogopogo, Bigfoot, Thunderbird, Twilight Mothman, Yeti, Nightcrawler, Cosmic Cthulhu, and the Jersey Devil.

Series Two features Griffin, Cerberus, Pegasus, Cactus Cat, Blue Dragon, Gargoyle, Wendigo, Kraken, Werewolf, Golden Dragon, Adlet, and Unicorn.

Founded in 2010, Cryptozoic's mission has been "fans first," as they strive to bring games, collectibles, trading cards, and more to the public.

©2019 Mel Cabre.

5

FACT OR FICTION?

Introduction

A religious pilgrimage gone wrong, a flying kangaroo, a fictional story turned legend, and a clash of worldviews. The stories we'll review in this chapter seem to have nothing in common but a fantastical element. But as the world of flying cryptids gifts us with historical content, it also offers life lessons and encourages us to question our worldviews. Each of these stories not only reminds us to be discerning but to have fun asking, What if . . . ?

The Lone Pine Mountain Devil

"My God. My God. They are all gone. The winged demons have risen! What sin have they committed against each other and thy sacred earth? May the forgiving Lord not abandon their souls, which were taken from them into the depths of hell! And through the earthly fires of man, a sole tree remained on the mountain's peak. And the devils that spared me returned to the refuge of the Lone Pine on the Mountain.'" Real or fiction, these are the words of Father Justus Martinez, the main character in the Lone Pine Mountain Devil Story. All good legends contain bits of fact, allowing for a proper suspension of disbelief and giving you the feeling that under the right circumstances, the unbelievable might be true.

The story of the Lone Pine Mountain Devil's slaughter of Father Martinez's traveling companions in the early twentieth century might have emerged from folktales settlers shared as they traveled the dangerous road westward. Or maybe it came from miners who told tall tales about horrendous events to scare away competition . . . or to explain the aftermath of horrendous scenes they stumbled upon in the wilderness. All plausible sources for the legend, but since the Lone Pine Mountain Devil story isn't found in newspaper archives, literature, journals of the time, or Native American lore, it appears to be the work of a creative mind who posted it on the internet sometime after the year 2000.

The big question is whether there is any truth to this story. While we can't prove or disprove its authenticity, we can explore the details to see what is plausible. If nothing else, looking for essential facts will add detail and lend credibility to this perfectly creepy story as you tell it around the campfire.

The Story

In 1878, Father Justus Martinez accompanied a stagecoach train of Spanish settlers through southern California. They were on their way to a Spanish mission about 110 miles north of San Diego. The cross-country road trip had been arduous, so the passengers agreed to stop and celebrate a feast to honor Saint Roderick, a Christian priest martyred for his faith.

The group of thirty-seven men, women, and children left their stagecoaches by the roadside and wound their way into a secluded area of the Sierra Nevada. At some point, the party stopped to celebrate, and things took a dark and wild turn. The reveling spun out of control. Unable to stop the riotous behavior, Father Martinez retreated to his tent on the outskirts of the encampment. As darkness set in, the celebration intensified into debauchery, and Father Martinez watched helplessly as people he had known and traveled with defiled God, nature, and themselves. Unattended, the fires also intensified and spread.

For weeks, workers at the mission had been on the lookout for the incoming settlers. Reports from stagecoach drivers indicated the group had left the road. They were nowhere to be found. Then one day, a weary traveler stumbled into the mission. His horse had run off, and the meager supplies he had salvaged were long gone. Father Justus Martinez had only the clothes on his back and his journal, in which he had written the account of his journey. Having sworn a vow of silence in the wake of the tragedy, the priest handed over the written account of what had happened. His words explained how "beasts damned by the good Lord" swarmed from the trees and attacked the settlers. The "winged demons" killed everyone.

Months later, it's said a team of copper miners discovered the rotting corpses of Father Martinez's traveling companions, with their faces and upper bodies mangled and flesh pulled from the bones. All the trees in the area had burned except for a single pine.

Winged Demons or Winged Dinosaurs?

Various descriptions of the Lone Pine Mountain Devil share these characteristics: carnivorous, bat-like, large, furry, multi-winged, razor sharp talons, and venomous fangs. Some believe it to be a West Coast relative of the Jersey Devil. Having read this far, you can make of that what you will.

Could the Lone Pine Mountain Devil have been a relict bird or flying dinosaur? Once living creatures with four wings would include the feathered dinosaurs *Microraptor* and *Sinornithosaurus*. According to the Natural History Museum in South Kensington, London, *Microraptor* was a small theropod about three feet long, weighing about 2.5 pounds. It had sharp pointy teeth, indicating it might have been carnivorous, and it is believed to have walked on two legs and to have been capable of gliding flight. While the description of the wing arrangement is a good match for the Lone Pine Mountain Devil, scientists have only found fossils of the *Microraptor* in China.

Closely related to *Microraptor* and about the same size is *Sinornithosaurus*, also found in China's fossil beds. *Sinornithosaurus* is thought to have had feathers attached to all four of its appendages, and there is speculation this dinosaur also glided.

In South America, *Andalgalornis*, also known as "terror birds," once roamed the continent devouring all sorts of prey. They possessed a pick-like beak, and scientists speculate they used this to repeatedly stab their prey. A second terror bird, *Llallawavis scagliai*, has recently been discovered, and according to Nicki Wilson for *BBC Earth*, this fossil gives more clues about terror birds' hunting style: "The joints between skull bones are fused, unlike other birds. . . . This rigidity would have been helpful with pummeling prey to death or using their head as a giant meat tenderizer. It would also provide the stable structure needed to rip flesh from bone."[2]

It feels safe to assume the Lone Pine Mountain Devil wasn't related to any of these ancient birds. While we can't prove these species didn't live in the untrod mountainous regions of California, it seems unlikely given the distribution of known fossils. But the existence of terror birds does present the possibility that fierce predatory birds of the nightmarish kind once lived.

What other species could have attacked from the air? While bats are not multi-winged, the rapid flapping of the two wings, outstretched from hand to back legs, might give the illusion of multiple sets of wings, especially in the dark. There are no bats known to live in the Sierra Nevada capable of mutilating thirty-seven people, but could the brown bats that do live there have become rabid and attacked humans? Symptoms of rabies would have presented in the first month and the infected humans would have died shortly thereafter, their bodies easy for wild animals to mutilate.

Spanish Immigration

The earliest recorded entrance by European Americans into the Sierra Nevada came between 1827 and 1833. A Spaniard by the name of Francisco Garces crossed the Colorado river into the state of Nevada as a missionary sent by the colonial Viceroyalty of New Spain, the territory including what we now call Mexico. He was assigned to explore the vast uncharted areas of the Great Basin, the desert east of the Sierra Nevada.

> **FUN FACT:** In 1776, the Spanish missionary Francisco Garces became the first European to meet the Mojave Indians and use their network of routes to cross the Mojave Desert. One of these trails became known as the Mojave Road and was used for stagecoach travel in the 1860s.

The California Gold Rush brought a large number of people into the western foothills of the Sierra Nevada from 1848 through 1855. Most people arrived by steamship. By 1870, California's population had surpassed

560,000. Migration to California continued in large waves, but, because of its inaccessibility, the Sierra Nevada was not fully explored until 1912, which explains how a small group of Catholic parishioners who entered the forests there in 1878 could easily have lost their way.

The story of the Lone Pine Mountain Devil claims the travelers had trekked across the continent. No one knows where they came from or why they left, nor do we know their final destination. There could have been several reasons to migrate in 1878, including prejudice from Protestant groups. Catholics were a relatively small minority until the 1840s when the Irish potato famine brought large numbers to America. Even then, Catholics were not readily accepted.

Nor were Mormons. Between 1848 and 1877, over one hundred thousand Mormons found their way through the mountains to Utah, settling in and around the Great Basin. Perhaps the Spanish convoy was starting their own non-conformist group, drawn together by their Catholic faith. Or maybe they traveled cross-country hoping to secure some of the plentiful agricultural jobs in southern California, where the communities embraced their culture.

Depending on their final destination, "cross continent" didn't necessarily mean east to west. They may have traveled north from Texas or Mexico or may conceivably have come south to escape the growing population in northern California. Regardless, stopping in the southern portion of the Sierra Nevada to escape the populated areas for a celebration seems plausible.

FUN FACT: James Gregory notes for the University of Washington's America's Great Migration Project that, even more than many states, California is a state of migrants: "California's history is keyed to migration. The most populous state in the union became so because so many people from other states and other lands have moved there. It was not until 2010 that the number of native-born Californians surpassed the number who had migrated from somewhere else. And still today most adults are from another state or another country."[3]

Spanish Missions

Alta California began as a province of New Spain in 1804 and included all of modern California, Nevada, and Utah, and parts of Arizona, Wyoming, Colorado, and New Mexico. King Carlos I gave control of the lands to the Franciscan College of San Fernando to claim the land for Spain. From 1769 to 1823, the Franciscans established twenty-one missions throughout Alta California. Following the Mexican War for Independence in 1822, the territory became a Mexican province for thirty-three years. In 1834, the mission system was abolished, and the land titled away to private parties. In 1855, after California became a state, the United States government declared private ownership of the missions unlawful and required they be returned to the Catholic church.

The legend says the mission Father Martinez's party was heading for was 110 miles north of San Diego. That would come in just south of Los Angeles, and the nearest mission would have been the San Juan Capistrano Mission. But the church at that site collapsed in an 1812 earthquake, and restoration did not begin until the late 1870s. It was probably not operable in 1878 when Father Justus Martinez made his trek out of the Sierra Nevada. It's more likely he would have traveled to San Gabriel Arcángel, which is about nine miles east of Los Angeles.

The Franciscans positioned San Gabriel at a confluence of three prominent trails. Settlers, military expeditions, and travelers frequently stayed at this mission. Founded in 1771 by the Blessed Junípero Serra, first father-president of the California missions, in conjunction with Fathers Pedro Benito Cambón and Angel Fernandez Somera y Balbuena, the mission housed over one thousand neophytes (converted Native Americans) during its peak occupancy in 1817. These neophytes spoke one of the Cupan languages of the Takic family and were called Gabrieleños after the mission. San Gabriel Arcángel would have been thriving in 1878. To this day, the church remains open to the public, and it is certainly plausible that a traveler from the Sierra Nevada would have found refuge here.

Was the Lone Pine in Lone Pine, California?

Present day Lone Pine, California, is located in Owens Valley, near the Alabama Hills, about sixteen miles southeast of Independence. The Lone Pine post office opened in 1870, and the town received its name from the solitary pine tree that once grew at the mouth of Lone Pine Canyon. In the early 1870s, Lone Pine was an important supply town for several nearby mining communities. The population grew to approximately 300 residents. On March 26, 1872, an earthquake destroyed most of the town and killed twenty-seven people.

While it's in the heart of copper mining territory, it seems unlikely this is the Lone Pine referred to in the story. Lone Pine, California, was founded eight years before the story took place, but it's located 230 miles north of the mission Father Justus Martinez walked to which was "110 miles north of San Diego." Why would the stage train travel that far north if three roads traveled through to the mission that was their destination?

Described as a weary, worn traveler who was weak, thirsty, and hungry when he arrived at the mission, Father Martinez does not appear to have encountered people or civilization as he walked to the mission, so the travelers were likely south of Death Valley near the Mojave Desert when they were killed. They couldn't have been much farther south, or they would no longer have been in the Sierra Nevada. To the north, no road existed that works within the context of this story. So Father Justus and crew were likely some distance from the current town of Lone Pine and the actual location of the massacre is unknown. This raises the question of how a group of copper miners could have found them.

Copper Mining

Copper was first discovered in California in 1840 in Los Angeles County. The Napoleon Mine at Copperopolis in Calaveras County opened in 1860 and was so productive that it ignited an economic boom from 1862 to 1866. The boom stimulated the development of copper mines along the "foothill copper belt," a 250-mile stretch of copper deposits in the Sierra Nevada foothills, running from Butte County in the northwest to Fresno County in the southeast. Production nearly ceased after 1868 when the shallow, oxidized ore was exhausted.

According to WesternMiningHistory.com there were no copper mining towns south of the Fresno area. If copper miners found the thirty-seven bodies, then it wasn't while they were working. Also, if the Spanish caravan camped near copper mines, then Father Martinez's walk to the mission "110 miles north of San Diego" would have been even farther out of the way than if they had camped near the town of Lone Pine.

One could assume that maybe miners of other types of minerals found the bodies. But to the south, the silver mining town of Calico and the tungsten mining town of Atolia had not yet been founded. They came about in the late 1880s and early 1900s. The gold mining town of Julian was booming in between Los Angeles and San Diego, but this mining town was closer to the coast, too far from the mountains for workers to "stumble" upon the bodies.

Saint Roderick

The group of Catholics were described as wanting to take a break from traveling to celebrate Saint Roderick. Also known as Ruderic or Rodriguez, Saint Roderick was a priest in Cabra, Spain, during an era of persecution of Christians by the Moors.

Roderick had two brothers: one Muslim and the other a fallen-away Catholic. One day, while these two were arguing, Roderick tried to stop them. The brothers turned on him and beat him unconscious. The Muslim brother then paraded Roderick through the streets proclaiming that he wished to become a Muslim. He also told the authorities that Roderick had converted to Islam. When Roderic awoke, he renounced his brother's story and told the authorities of his loyalty to the Catholic faith. The authorities accused Roderick of apostasy. After a long imprisonment, they beheaded him on March 13, AD 857.

In remembrance of Saint Roderick, Catholics feast on March 13 and give thanks for their freedom to worship without persecution. Stopping to honor the saint and enjoy a respite from travel sounds plausible. A feast escalating into a wild, out-of-control celebration isn't impossible to imagine either. More difficult to imagine is the swooping in of demon-like birds to punish the revelers. Even if we assume there were flying creatures capable of attacking and killing people in the area, it's hard to believe their motivation was punishment as suggested in the priest's journal. Ascribing a punishment motive to flying demons seems like an unwarranted assumption.

FUN FACT: "There's a parallel between religious experience and horror," writes John Morehead; blogger, researcher, and speaker in intercultural studies. "In reality, religion embodies both the horrifying and the positive."[4] Utilizing this good and evil battle in storytelling adds an additional layer of fear and awe.

Also difficult to believe is the absence of publicity. Finding thirty-seven people slaughtered would have be significant and alarming. In 1878, California newspapers were in full swing. This would have been a major story and Father Justus Martinez's journal would likely have been quoted long before an internet post in the 2000s. But you can be the judge of whether this story is fact or fiction, and enjoy the retelling nevertheless.

Phenomenal Week

January 16–23, 1909, was the week the Jersey Devil became famous. Nearly every household in South Jersey heard about the monstrous, flying creature that was roaming through their neighborhoods, leaving thousands of hoofprints in his wake. The newswires picked up the stories and transported them across the country. The public at large became consciously aware that a monster was on the loose.

To this day, no one knows whether man or beast made all of those hoofprints. It seems impossible that every hoofprint and eyewitness account was part of even an elaborate hoax. But if they weren't part of the hoax, where did all those hoofprints come from?

How the Story Begins

Late Saturday night on January 16, 1909, a resident in Woodbury, New Jersey, claimed he heard hissing on his property. While looking into the source of the noise, he saw a white flash and red eyes. Slightly northeast in Bristol, Pennsylvania, more sightings occurred along with several hoof-like prints. When Sunday morning dawned with a fresh blanket of snow, rumors of the Leeds Devil's return had spread throughout the community.

Tuesday, January 19, in Gloucester City, a Mr. and Mrs. Nelson Evans woke to strange noises. When they peered out the bedroom window, they saw an odd creature walking across the roof of their shed.

> It was about three feet and a half high, with a head like a collie dog and a face like a horse. It had a long neck, wings about two feet long, and its back legs were like those of a crane, and it had horse's hooves. It walked on its back legs and held up two short front legs with paws.[5]

Mr. Nelson shared his story with the *Philadelphia Evening Bulletin* resulting in the now famous Jersey Devil Strip from 1909.

Wednesday, January 20, the *Trenton Evening Times* printed another Leeds Devil story, "Fly Rival of 'Leeds Devil' Has Jersey People Frightened," spreading the news of hoofprints found in Burlington and Gloucester counties. The article said the creature was two-legged, with hooves like a horse, had wings, and could fly. The creature was also small enough to crawl through a hole less than a foot in diameter and was cat-like because it could walk on top of fences and over chicken coops. The article goes on to compare this information to those of previous Leeds Devil sightings.

As more newspaper articles ran stories about the reemergence of the Leeds Devil, the public grew concerned. Little did they know a plot that depended heavily on public hysteria was nefariously unfolding.

The New Jersey What-Is-It. First published in the Philadelphia Evening Bulletin on Wednesday, January 20, 1909. Photo in public domain.

The Ninth and Arch Street Dime Museum

The Ninth and Arch Street Dime Museum, which had entertained the public with spectacles and oddities under Charles A. Bradenbaugh's steerage since 1885, faced financial disaster. It was up to the publicity agent, Norman Jeffries, and business manager, T. F. Hopkins, to devise a plan that would regenerate the public's interest. If they failed, they would all lose their jobs.

Even with formerly popular acts like the Skeleton Man, the Human Bat, and the Glass Eater, the museum was losing the interest of the gawking public. But when hoofprints and rumors stirred curiosity, Jeffries and Hopkins saw an opportunity to play on their strengths and take advantage of the growing frenzy amongst the people of the greater Philly area. They discussed how to make the creature visible to all. If they had a body, no one would be able to resist a ten-cent glimpse.

While Jeffries and Hopkins plotted about how to engineer such a creature, area newspapers took part in their own sport of one-upmanship with clever, comical, and slightly ridiculous copy. In January 2019, Joseph A. Gambardello of the *Philadelphia Inquirer* offered this perspective on the Jersey Devil sightings: "Two things should be kept in mind when reading the old stories about the Devil. First is that journalistic standards in those days were, to say the least, loose, and newspapermen often did favors that were reciprocated with free meals or theater tickets or bottles of booze at Christmas.

"Second is that in the face of fierce competition, newspapers would seek to match stories in rival publications at any cost—even if the price was the truth.

"With newspapers carrying stories of witnesses seeing the creature on both sides of the Delaware River from Trenton to the Delaware Bay, the fight was on. Somewhere in the mix was Norman Jeffries filing reports to willing recipients."[6]

Some excerpts from newspaper accounts may help give an idea of the tone. On Friday, January 22, 1909, the *Philadelphia Inquirer* explained what kind of creature was on the loose.

VAMPIRE MISSING; LOOK OUT, JERSEY

Australian Wonder, Cross Between a Kangaroo and Bat, Strangely Disappears
May be the "Flying Devil" That Has So Vexed Good Folk Across Delaware

The monster's feet don't seem to scan,
They're like Walt Whitman's lines—

You've got to analyze the words
and not regard the signs.

The article itself reads, "The freak making so much a disturbance in New Jersey just now is said to be an Australian waif. . . . He has performed stunts that might not have been considered conventional. Over in Woodbury, the people are almost in a state of hysteria. . . . John North was in the very act of going after his gun when a huge Maltese cat, a member of the family, appeared and said, 'Don't shoot!' It didn't say this in so many words but North approved it. . . . A woman's meeting was broken up in South Westville because one of the members thought she saw 'it.' As soon as this fact became known, all the husbands in that section laid aside their guns and went out with salt in their hands, hoping for an opportunity to put it on the monster's tail."

In what appears to be a whimsical response to the wild Australian vampire theory (and other claims), *The Evening World* out of New York published an article on January 22, 1909, that we've left mostly intact for entertainment.

Jersey Devil Is Classified As A "Bombat."

It Flies, Swims, Eats Hay, Chews Cud and Lays Red, White and Blue Eggs.
 Eggs are Explosive
 Full Moon Bursts 'Em, So the "Thing" Makes Its Nest in Extinct Craters
 Although the press agent of J. H. Hope, the animal dealer, of No. 35 North Ninth Street, Philadelphia, has been put under bonds to keep the peace and stop sending out descriptions of the "Australian vampire devil," which he declares strayed from the zoological freak nursery of his employer, and notwithstanding that ten warrants charging criminal mendacity have been asked for in Burlington County, N.J., there still poured into the Quaker City to-day a multitude of hot-scented weird, lurid, hallucinatory, phantasmagoric and preternatural descriptions of the "Thing" that is loose in the applejack belt of South Jersey and the schnapps district of Pennsylvania.
 "It's a Bombat."
 There is no doubt that all that populous country is subject to an uncanny visitation, but in the interest of science some sort of restraint must be put on the testimony that is accumulating concerning the features, habits, inclination and disposition of the "Whatever-is-it?"
 The Zoological League of West Philadelphia issued a bulletin to-day declaring, in sober, academic terms, that there is every reason to believe that the "Thing" is a Bombat. And a Bombat, bear in mind, is not a mythical fanciful creature of the Jabberwock and Snark type. It is a recognized, tabulated, tagged and categorized monster that occupies an important classification in abnormal zoology.

The writer then offers the scientific description of a Bombat. The author, who calls himself a paleontologist, attempts to reason out what people are seeing. He continues:

> The fact the Bombat lays a red, white and blue egg has lent some slight color to the contention of the ornithologists, but the further fact that the Bombat's egg explodes when the moon is full offers a problem ornithology cannot solve. Darwin stated in the suppressed addenda of his third edition of the "Origin of the Species," that the Bombat was remotely evolved from the Hippodot, which would account for its horse-like profile and cloven hoofs, but in my paleontological research, I have been unable to unearth one authentic fragment of a Hippodot. In the Dusseldorf museum there is a paleontological exhibit that is claimed to have been the left wing of a Hippodot. I have examined this under a microscope, but can find no Bombat markings. . . . The Bombat, when erect, stands about three feet six inches high, has a four-foot spread of wing, the duplicate vertebrae of a pterodactyl, fur around its neck and scales on its tail. It has no certain habitat and does not propagate extensively, because of the explosive nature of the eggs. Only one in every sixty-nine eggs of the Bombat is successfully hatched, and these, I have observed, are laid in the craters of volcanoes, where they are protected from the moonlight. The average age of a wombat is 311 years. They are difficult to capture and their bite is fatal. I expect to have further data on the Bombat in my next edition. . . . The Recording Secretary of the West Philadelphia Zoological League impresses upon the lay mind in the second bulletin that the Bombat is in no way related to the wombat. . . . Moreover, declares this bulletin, the perfervid efforts of the part of dealer Hope's press agent to confuse the Bombat with the alleged vampire that strayed out of Mr. Hope's cages is puerile in its futility. A vampire is merely a South American blood-sucking bat of the genera Desmodus and Diphylia. There is absolutely nothing desmodine or diphylian about a Bombat.

This column, obviously written as satire, implies Jeffries wrote the *Philadelphia Inquirer* article about the vampire bat, but ironically the two pieces were published on the same day.

As the hoaxers hoped, continued reports and publicity had their desired effect. Many people refused to leave their homes. Schools closed, employees missed work, and social functions were cancelled. The Philadelphia Zoo offered a $10,000 reward for the capture of the creature. The public had been primed. Now it was time for the final act.

Sometime during the week, Jeffries and Hopkins had contacted animal trainer Jacob Hope and shared their plan. Hope produced an animal that fit their description: a living kangaroo, upon which they painted stripes and attached a pair of homemade wings. Jeffries hired a Ringling Brothers Circus clown named George Hartzell to round up some friends to act as monster hunters. They trekked into the wilds of Philadelphia's Fairmount Park and caught the gruesome creature. The next day—Saturday, January 23—the *Philadelphia Inquirer* reported the capture, stating the fearsome beast was a cross between "a kangaroo and an Australian water bird." An ad appeared in the paper, announcing that the captured Leeds Devil would be on display.

> 9TH AND ARCH MUSEUM
> T. F. Hopkins, Manager
> Caught!!! And Here!!! Alive!!!
> THE LEEDS DEVIL
> Captured Friday After a
> Terrific Struggle
> Exhibited Exclusively Here At
> $1000.00 A Week
> The Fearful, Frightful, Ferocious Monster Which
> Has been Terrorizing Two States.
> Swims! Flys! Gallops!
> Exhibited Securely Chained
> In a Massive Steel Cage.
> A LIVING DRAGON
> More Fearsome than the Fabled Monsters
> of Mythology
> Don't Miss The
> Sight of a Lifetime

Thousands came out to see the monster. Surrounding newspapers ran articles about the beast and its capture. More sightings occurred with descriptions that now resembled "a winged-kangaroo." But the effort only worked to keep the museum's doors open a few more weeks. No matter the ruse or trickery, the day of the dime museum had passed.

Looking back on Jeffries' role in the 1909 appearances of the Jersey Devil, Joseph Gambardello of the *Philadelphia Enquirer* writes: "Years later, Jeffries, whose name also appears as Jefferies in newspaper clips, confessed to staging the stunt. When he died at the age of sixty-seven (or fifty-seven, according to the New York Times), the [Philadelphia] *Inquirer* said, 'Reports that the Jersey Devil had reappeared aroused his showman instinct and he used all the arts of a press agent to build up the belief in the legend.'"[7]

But where did the initial hoofprints come from if not from Jeffries and his men? Were they planted by a random hoaxer, looking for some fun after a fresh snowfall? Or, were they made by something else? Perhaps an elusive creature that sought refuge in the surrounding forests after those first couple of days? Fact or fiction, people reported seeing the Leeds Devil before Jeffries entered the ruckus. It is disappointing that because of the hoax, we are farther than ever from the truth.

The Power of Mass Hysteria

In an article on mass hysteria for *Psychology Today*, UCLA professor of psychiatry Gary Small describes the way our minds and bodies can get in an escalating feedback loop when we are faced with hard-to-interpret and frightening situations: "When we face uncertainty, our minds crave explanations. If we have no way to account for symptoms, we feel out of control and our fear escalates. And, if we learn that our own minds may have caused these very real symptoms, we tend to feel more anxiety about what our minds might do next. People may worry that their brains are possessed by some outside spirit, or perhaps a poltergeist has taken charge of their willpower. They'd rather latch onto something."[8] Even if that something is a flying kangaroo-bird.

> **FUN FACT:** In December 1997, the 38th episode of Pokémon never aired outside Japan after nearly 12,000 children complained of nausea and seizures. The episode, "Dennō Senshi Porygon" (aka "Cyber Soldier Porygon") featured bright flashing lights and rapid changes in colors. The incidence of photosensitive epilepsy is estimated at only 1 in 5,000, which is why some believe this was a case of mass hysteria.

Often, the success of anything depends on timing, who you know, and the alignment of the sun, moon, and stars. Public curiosity, the press, and the exploitive tactics of Norman Jeffries catapulted the Jersey Devil into stardom for one phenomenal week, sealing his station in New Jersey Culture as equal parts lurking cryptid and pop culture icon.

The Piasa (pie-a-saw)—"The Bird That Eats Men"

One of the first written descriptions of the Piasa Bird comes from Father Jacques Marqette, who came upon a depiction of it on a cliff high above the waters of the Mississippi River in 1763:

> While Skirting some rocks, which by Their height and Length inspired awe, We saw upon one of them two painted monsters which at first made Us afraid, and upon Which the boldest savages dare not Long rest their eyes. They are as

large As a calf; they have Horns on their heads Like those of deer, a horrible look, red eyes, a beard Like a tiger's, a face somewhat like a man's, a body Covered with scales, and so Long A tail that it winds all around the Body, passing above the head and going back between the legs, ending in a Fish's tail. Green, red, and black are the three Colors composing the Picture. Moreover, these 2 monsters are so well painted that we cannot believe that any savage is their author; for good painters in france would find it difficult to paint so well,—and, besides, they are so high up on the rock that it is difficult to reach that place Conveniently to paint them. Here is approximately The shape of these monsters, As we have faithfully Copied It.⁹

Father Jacques Marquette S.J. (1637–1675) was a French-born missionary who moved to New France (modern-day Quebec) in 1666 at the age of twenty-nine to interact with and teach the indigenous people. Two years after his arrival, he moved up the St. Lawrence River to help found Sault Ste. Marie, the earliest European settlement in Michigan. Marquette also founded missions at St. Ignace, Michigan, and La Pointe, Wisconsin. It was at La Pointe that he learned about the trading opportunities along the Mississippi River. He spoke with his superiors who were hopeful he might find a water passage to the Pacific.

On May 13, 1673, Marquette set out with fur-trader Louis Jolliet and a team of several men in canoes to explore the upper Mississippi River valley. While they confirmed the river fed into the Gulf, they did not find a westward passage. The crew traveled as far as Arkansas, where they encountered Native Americans with Spanish goods. Fearing an encounter with Spanish explorers, the crew turned around and followed the Mississippi back to the mouth of the Illinois River. It was in this area, where the Missouri, Mississippi, and Illinois Rivers come together near the town presently known as Alton, Illinois, that our story takes place.

The Story

What follows is a summary of an 1836 story "The Piasa: An Indian Tradition of Illinois" by John Russell, printed in *The Family Magazine*:

> Many years before the Europeans arrived, when the *Megalonyx* and mastodons still roamed the earth, there existed a bird large enough to carry off a deer. This bird developed a taste for human flesh and would prey on nothing else. Skilled in hunting and very fast, the bird would dive in without warning, snatch up his human prey, and then return to his cave in the bluffs where he would devour his meal.
>
> Whole villages were being depleted. The Illini chief, Ouatoga, knew he must come up with a solution or his people would be lost forever. He left his tribe for a month and fasted, praying to the Great Spirit for help. On the last night of his fast, the Great Spirit appeared to him in a dream and instructed him to select twenty of his warriors. Each one should return to the bluff carrying a bow with a poisoned-tipped arrow and hide out of sight. One warrior should stand out in the open as bait for the Piasa. Upon the bird's arrival, the men were to shoot it. The chief thanked the Great Spirit and returned to his people, relaying his dream.
>
> After selecting the men, they returned to the bluff and hid out of sight. Ouatoga stood alone, in the open, sacrificing himself. As he began the death chant of a warrior, the monstrous bird swooped in. Giant talons reached toward the chief. Twenty arrows flew through the air and pierced the creature. The Piasa screeched wildly and then fell to the ground, dead.
>
> To honor the Great Spirit, the Native Americans painted the Piasa on the face of the bluff.

After telling the story, Russell went on to write that he wasn't certain of its validity. But he then described his visit to a cave on top of the bluff.

> The cave was extremely difficult of access, and at one point of our progress I stood at an elevation of more than one hundred and fifty feet on the face of the bluff, with barely room to sustain one foot. The unbroken wall towered

above me, while below was the river. After a long and perilous clambering we reached the cave, which was about fifty feet above the surface of the river. . . . The roof of the cavern was vaulted, the top of which was hardly less than twenty-five feet in height. The shape was irregular, but so far as I could judge, the bottom would average twenty by thirty feet. The floor of this cave throughout its whole extent was a mass of human bones. Sculls and other bones were mingled together in the utmost confusion. . . . We dug to the depth of three or four feet in every quarter of the cavern and still we found only bones.[10]

Today, the painting of the Piasa Bird has been recreated twice, to ensure a record of the image it is not lost to history. The newer pieces of artwork show wings, but Marquette did not allude to wings on the creature he described. An oversight? No one knows.

Origins in the Past

Archeologists have discovered evidence of an early Mississippian period settlement about twenty miles south of the Piasa mural, near St. Louis, on the Illinois side of the river. They believe this early civilization, called Cahokia, existed between AD 1000 and AD 1350. At the height of its development around the year AD 1100, archeologists believe somewhere between ten thousand and twenty thousand people lived at the settlement. Marquette and Joliet did not meet any Native Americans in the area when they came through in 1673, but on a visit to the Cahokia Mounds State Historic site in October of 2019, William Iseminger, assistant director of the location, informed the authors that a few decades later, "French settlers and priests settled about twelve miles south of this site and established their village next to a tribe called Cahokia and named their village after them." These Cahokia were descendants of the Illinwek, an ancient Algonquian speaking tribe now known as the Illini. According to Iseminger, "They did not build mounds and did not know who did. By the 1730s, the French and Cahokia were not getting along very well so the French and priests from the Seminary of Foreign Missions moved the Cahokia north to the Cahokia Mounds site and built a chapel for them on the first terrace of the massive mound at the center of the site, where they established their new village until the 1750s.

"Much later, from 1809 to 1813, a group of French Trappist Monks settled on a mound near the large one and planted orchards and crops on its [the large mound's] terraces. Local people then began to call the large mound 'Monks Mound.'"

Because of the Cahokia Mounds' positions near the three rivers, the early inhabitants may have built one of the largest and most influential urban settlements of the Mississippian culture. The people were masters at constructing large earthen structures and operated under an organized government that archeologists believe represents a Mississippian religion that first evolved at Cahokia and then spread via migration throughout the south, influencing communities in Texas, Oklahoma, Louisiana, Alabama, Georgia, and Florida.

Animal pictographs were common motifs among the Cahokia. Is it possible it was the Cahokia who created a barely accessible pictograph of the Piasa monster? The Cahokia Mounds State Historic Site, which originally included 120 mounds and was recognized as a World Heritage Site by UNESCO in 1982 for its importance in the understanding of Native American Prehistory, uses a sandstone "Birdman" as their logo.

Perhaps the Cahokia placed the Piasa Bird strategically along the river to warn strangers they were entering Cahokia territory. Or maybe they were showing respect to the serpent monster—a spirit similar to the "great horned serpent" or "underwater panther" found in the mythology of other tribes, which they believed was responsible for dangerous waters by the whipping of its long tail. While these spirits were considered dangerous and strongly avoided in most circumstances, favor could be obtained by showing respect—a desirable asset as one traveled the "great river" and navigated its many dangers.

Cahokia's population began to decline by AD 1200, and by AD 1350, the settlement was essentially abandoned, possibly because of warfare, political instability, climate change and droughts, or simply because of a change in lifestyle. By the early seventeenth century, many pre-Columbian tribes were undergoing significant changes and relocations. Algonquian tribes migrated westward to put distance between themselves and their Iroquois enemies. When Europeans started coming through the area, the Illini inhabited most of the territory around present day Alton and much of the central Mississippi Valley and Illinois River valley.

At some point after French exploration of the Mississippi began, the original Piasa rock art crumbled into an unrecognizable form. It was recreated by William Dennis in 1825. He painted the mural in a more accessible location and is speculated to be the one who added wings (although no one knows if the original had wings). He labeled the creation the "Flying Dragon." Then in 1870, a quarry company blasted away the entire rock

The Birdman Tablet. Photo used with permission, courtesy of the Cahokia Mounds State Historic Site.

Engraved on sandstone, . . . [an] artifact was found in the 100-foot tall Monk's Mound and is thought to represent an anthropomorphic bird deity. The Bird-man tablet depicts a man wearing a bird-like mask with a hooked beak, holding a wing up to one side in a dancing posture. The reverse side has cross-hatching thought to represent snakeskin. Thus the tablet portrays creatures of the three spiritual realms: Upper World—Bird; Middle or This World—Man; Lower World—Snake/Serpent.

upon which the pictograph appeared. Citizens of Alton sketched the "Flying Dragon" as they remembered it and repainted the image on a cliff face in 1924 along the Great River Road above Alton.

It was eleven years after William Dennis created his "Flying Dragon" depiction that John Russell, a professor of Greek and Latin at Shurtleff College in Upper Alton, Illinois published his article called, "The Piasa" in *The Family Magazine*. Upon questioning, Russell admitted the entire story and cave of bones were a product of his imagination.

The Piasa Monster. Alton, Illinois. ©2019 Mel Cabre.

Even so, Marquette had described the cliff mural and the Native Americans' reactions to it long before John Russell wrote his story. In more recent history, witnesses have reported large bird sightings and attacks in Illinois. Could this mean there is some element of truth to Russell's tale? From water serpent to flying dragon to Piasa Monster, the cliffs above Alton, Illinois, tell a story—some fact and some fiction, but all of it in remembrance of a sky monster forever embedded in Illinois history.

The Word Piasa

Thomas Hutchins (1730–1789), surveyor and our foremost American geographer, created a 1778 map titled, "A new map of the western parts of Virginia, Pennsylvania, Maryland, and North Carolina; comprehending the river Ohio, and all the rivers, which fall into it; part of the river Mississippi, the whole of the Illinois River." On the map, Hutchins labels present day Alton, Illinois with the name "*PIASAS*." This map is one of the earliest documented references to the word Piasa. But it may have been a corrup-

tion of a different word. Twenty years later, French explorer, Nicolas De Finiels, called the riverbed area *Hauteurs des Palissades*, which translates to "heights of the palisades."

Quest for the Ropen

What Is a Ropen?

For years, reports of living pterosaurs have come out of Papua New Guinea and its surrounding islands. Of particular interest is a creature said to live on Umboi Island which is just off the mainland coast. Locals have reported sightings of a creature they call *Duwas* or *Ropen*. With a wingspan said to be up to twenty-nine feet, the dark-gray flyer possesses two leathery, bat-like wings and a long tail with a diamond-shape on the end. Also noted is a head crest and dermal bump, a tooth-filled beak, and razor-sharp claws.

Cryptozoologists believe the Ropen emerged from either the *Dimorph-odon* or *Rhamphorhynchus* lineages. *Dimorphodons* were only about three feet long with a wingspan nearing five feet. They were named for having two distinct types of teeth in their skull. The tail of *Dimorphodon* was long, with thirty vertebrae of varying lengths, and may or may not have had a widened tail tip like that found on *Rhamphorhynchus*. No impressions of one have been found to date. *Rhamphorhynchus* was slightly smaller than *Dimorphodon* and had a long, narrow skull and teeth that pointed forward. Fossils impressions of *Rhamphorhynchus*'s long tail show it clearly ended in a diamond-shaped tip.

The Ropen is far larger than either of these extinct pterosaurs. It is thought to be nocturnal and give off a bioluminescent glow. As reported on Paul Nation's Indava Bird Project website, locals call the light *Indava*, which means, "Bird that flies at night and brings death."[11]

Johnathan Whitcomb is a leading cryptozoologist involved in the Papua New Guinea pterosaur investigations. Also a private investigative journalist and forensic court videographer, he has devoted more than ten thousand hours to investigating the Ropen and interviewing witnesses. Whitcomb studied the Ropen's lights and found they moved toward the coast early at night and returned inland later. This aligned with the reports of locals, who say the Ropens fly out to the reef at night to feed and then return to their resting places in the mountains.

Whitcomb published his findings in *Creation Research Science Quarterly*, where he garnered respect for his attention to detail. As is usual for cryptozoologists, his work was met with skepticism, but in addition there were personal attacks. Whitcomb and other biblically grounded cryptozoologists have been the targets of cynical, unkind, and even hateful remarks. In this chapter the big question is not whether the Ropen exists, but why this cryptid has caused dissension outside the world of cryptozoology. But first, we need to explore the Ropen story to provide context.

Where It Began

In 2005, Ropen investigator and explorer Garth Guessman interviewed eyewitness Duane Hodgkinson while fellow investigator Johnathan Whitcomb filmed the exchange. In the video, Hodgkinson talks about his unexpected Ropen sighting in 1944. Hodgkinson had been stationed in Finschhafen, New Guinea, with the U.S. military. While there, he made several trips into some of the surrounding native villages with a friend and a native guide.

In the interview, Hodgkinson reported they had been walking along a trail about noon on a clear day. The group came upon a large clearing of grass about two feet high. A thrashing in the brush came from one edge of the clearing. The men paused, and a large creature "ran to their left, taking six to ten steps" before it ascended at an angle of about 30 degrees. It disappeared over the dense brush but soon returned and flew over the clearing, presenting a perfect side view of its features before flying out of sight.

The tail had been approximately ten to fifteen feet, and the wingspan about twenty-nine feet. It had a long neck, and a long appendage off the back of its head. Hodgkinson said he was so focused on the head crest that he didn't notice if there was anything at the end of the tail. A certified flight instructor with over thirteen thousand hours of flight time, Hodgkinson likened the bird's wingspan to the Piper Tri-Pacer he owned.[12]

Hodgkinson's testimony, along with Ropen reports from others investigating sightings of possible pterosaurs, inspired Johnathan Whitcomb to conduct his own expedition. He hoped to gather video evidence of a "living pterodactyl." While he didn't obtain video during his expedition on Umboi Island in 2004, Whitcomb interviewed several people who had seen the Ropen. He came to this conclusion:

> Only after I had left Umboi Island and was leaving for the mainland of Papua New Guinea did I suddenly realize something I never before expected. All the sightings correlated very well with the idea that a single giant pterosaur lived on the island. There is no sign that there's a colony of Ropens. Breeding may take place on a much larger island nearby, but the Ropen of Umboi Island is an individual creature with its own territory.[13]

Papua New Guinea and Umboi Island

Formed by volcanic activity and surrounded by beautiful coral reefs and beaches, Papua New Guinea lies between Australia and the Philippines. The country comprises the eastern half of the island of New Guinea (the second largest island in the world) and several smaller islands. The entire nation covers 178,704 square miles and has an estimated population of only about 8.7 million people, making Papua New Guinea one of the most sparsely populated countries in the world. Along with many groups of uncontacted people, researchers believe there may be a wealth of undiscovered species of plants and animals in the interior's unexplored and richly diverse jungles.

Umboi Island is positioned between mainland Papua New Guinea and the Island of New Britain. It's here that many locals have seen the Ropen lights flying to or from the larger mountains. Some describe the light as lasting about five seconds.

FUN FACT: During World War II, the New Guinea campaign (1942–1945) was a protracted and deadly military campaign among the conflicts between Japan and the Allies. During the three years of the campaign, approximately 216,000 Japanese, Australian, and U.S. servicemen lost their lives. What we now know as the Independent State of Papua New Guinea was created after the Allies won the war and combined the Territories of Papua and New Guinea.[14]

From the First Sightings to the Present

Lucy Evelyn Cheesman was an entomologist who curated insects for the London Zoo. She went on eight solo expeditions in the South Pacific and collected over seventy thousand specimens. While in Papua New Guinea, she witnessed unusual lights that moved across the sky, lasting for only four to five seconds, and wrote about them in her book *The Two Roads of Papua* (1935).

Later, local people shared stories about the Ropen with missionaries and sparked the interest of young earth creationists such as Paul Nation, Johnathan Whitcomb, and Garth Guessman. These men led several expeditions and conducted dozens of interviews throughout the 1990s and 2000s. Many residents reported seeing large, featherless birds and lights in the night sky.

One of the most notable of these interviews occurred during a visit in 2004, when pterosaur investigator Johnathan Whitcomb spoke to a man named Gideon and two other witnesses who said they (and others) had climbed up a mountain to a volcanic crater lake not far from their village in the west central area of Umboi Island. There they said they saw the Ropen fly over the lake and described the long tail with a diamond shape on the end.

On his website "Pterosaurs Still Living," Whitcomb writes about his conversation with Gideon. The Umboi resident likened the mouth or beak of the Ropen to that of a crocodile. Gideon continued drawing the body with a series of bumps or scale ridges that ran down the neck, back, and tail.

He agreed the wings were like that of a flying fox and described the tail as about twenty-three feet long with no feathers.

Cryptozoologist Paul Nation has documented his five expeditions to Papua New Guinea to study the Ropen on his webpage, IndavaBird.com. In 2006, he traveled for four days, deep into the rainforest. During this expedition, he photographed a yellowish glow that moved across the sky and disappeared near a volcanic peak. Computer enhancement of video he took convinced Nation the lights were not manmade.

In 2015, field researchers Milt Marcy and Peter Beach also led an expedition to Umboi Island. In the village where they stayed, elders shared stories about long-ago encounters with pterosaurs. One story told of a time when someone shot a pterosaur using a missionary's gun, and the meat, cooked in three large pots, fed the entire village.

During their expedition, Marcy and Beach captured video of a large flying creature resembling a pterosaur or frigatebird. Frigatebirds live along coastal waters in the tropics and subtropics and can soar for long periods. They have distinctive bent wings and long forked tails used to steer. Because of the distance, specific details were hard to discern, and the flyer remains unidentified.[15]

A Clash of Worldviews

Whether their sightings are of sky monsters, Bigfoot, Dogman, or the Ogopogo, eyewitnesses are hesitant to share their experiences outside of the cryptid subculture for fear of ridicule. However, that doesn't diminish the impact of the life-altering encounters. When a person whole-heartedly believes what they saw, their worldview shifts to accommodate a new reality. Because that reality differs from the norm, eyewitnesses often become researchers and investigators to understand what they witnessed and prove it was real.

As noted above, some of the investigators had encounters, others did not. So what has driven Christian cryptozoologists to study the Ropen and devote thousands of hours to website construction, expeditions to remote locations, interviewing witnesses, and writing books and articles?

In his 2012 book *The Undefeated Mind*, Alex Lickerman, MD, talks about passion. Passion drives our wants and is the fuel that feeds our motivation. In an article for *Psychology Today*, Lickerman writes: "The word itself, 'passion,' derives from the Latin root 'pati'—which means 'to suffer.'

The veracity in this linguistic statement lies in the fact that passion is what moves you to persevere at something despite fear, unhappiness or pain. It is the determination and motivation to push through suffering for the sake of an end goal."[16]

But not everyone shares the same passion. Type Ropen into a search engine and you'll see two types of articles—those written by cryptozoologists and those that refute, and, on occasion, attack the cryptozoologists. There are few moderate responses.

As discussed in chapter 4, our worldview (the way we interpret our surroundings) influences how we perceive information. A biblical creationist will interpret information based on six days of creation by God. Many believe in a young earth (about six thousand years old). An evolutionary biologist, who interprets information based on the big bang theory and the theory of evolution, measures the earth's age in billions of years. Of course, many fall somewhere in the middle, and are able to reconcile a bit of both theories. Others believe in a different theory all together.

Cryptozoologists of any faith—or no faith at all—are passionate in their beliefs. It rolls with the territory. As with any human, worldview influences the interpretation of data. While critical thinking is important to test and understand belief systems, rudeness (which includes snarkiness and cynicism)—even as subtext—serves no beneficial purpose.

Consider a social media post like the following: "Creationism (or Evolution) is garbage. Only simple-minded people believe in it." Soon a battle "for" and "against" ensues in the comments sections. What makes people choose confrontational words? In his *Psychology Today* article, Dr. Lickerman continues: "Our conscious minds aren't so much in charge of the decisions we make as they are great rationalizers of . . . [our wants]. Which means they often collude with our unconscious minds to craft stories about why we do things and even why we feel things that are just blatantly untrue. We often have far more invested in seeing ourselves as virtuous, noble, fair-minded, and good than we do in recognizing the truth: that we often want things and therefore do things that make us base, selfish, self-righteous, and unjust."

To change potentially offensive or rash behavior, we need to address our deep-seated, unconscious needs. This may keep us from acting on our conscious wants and desires. Dr. Lickerman suggests that "pausing to ask yourself just what exactly you want—not what you think you should want or what others want you to want or want for you—without judgment can often be a surprisingly emotional exercise."

But are our wants obtainable? If they are not (such as changing someone else's belief system), then proceed with caution. We must filter passion (those heated feelings that want to rip off a nasty reply) with understanding and self-control so our reaction doesn't set off a blaze of unkindness that hurts people. If the want is to hurt or attack, recognize that consciously, and then dig deeper. What drives your passionate feeling? Tackle that issue, because it may have little to do with your immediate want.

In his book *Big Bird! Modern Sightings of Flying Monsters* (2000), cryptozoologist Ken Gerhard devotes an entire chapter to sightings of *Pteranodon*-type animals in Africa, New Guinea, Australia, Asia, and even Europe. He reports objectively on the young earth creationists' point of view by focusing on eyewitness accounts and available information. While his beliefs and worldview may differ from other investigators and cryptozoologists, Gerhard doesn't let it stop him. His efforts result in fun and poignant content that allows the reader to decipher the truth for themselves. This objective approach not only encourages a larger audience, it effectively shows off his research skills.

6

WHO'S WHO IN THE SKY AROUND THE WORLD?

Sightings of flying cryptids happen all over the world and these creatures are reported in a wide variety of shapes, sizes, and locations. We can't investigate them all, but in this chapter we have compiled a field guide to some of the more notable cryptids we have not covered in depth so far. As we've organized their profiles, we've tried not to repeat a creature we've discussed elsewhere in the book unless the context provides new information. We've written about the sightings of Mothman in Point Pleasant, West Virgina, for example, and a similar creature has been reported in Germany as the Freiburg Shrieker. Because the basic design and context of the cryptids were similar, we left the Freiburg Shrieker out of this section (although we mention him in chapter 2). Conversely, the Kongamato is described as very much like the Thunderbirds we've discussed elsewhere, but the context of the sighting provides new information.

Cryptid enthusiasts will note that many of these creatures have made appearances in the United States, but their origin or the story that put them on the map comes from another country. Our list isn't exhaustive, and, as in chapter 2, we pulled information from a variety of eyewitness sightings and compiled the most common characteristics.

We've indulged ourselves by highlighting a few flying creatures from legends and local folklore. While these creatures exist only in the fictional world, at some level, they usually embody an element of cultural truth. We found them fascinating and wanted to share.

AHOOL

Wingspan Eighteen to twenty-eight feet.

Physical Description Giant bat or flying primate. Two to three feet in body length; covered in short, dark grey fur; black eyes; enormous claws at the top of forearms.

Demeanor Territorial, may be aggressive toward humans, mainly eats fish.

Location The jungles of Java and New Guinea, Indonesia.

Notes Named after the noise it makes: "aHOOoool." First noted sighting occurred in 1925 when Dr. Ernest Bartels explored a waterfall in the Salek Mountains. Also known as Athol.

ALICANTO

Physical Description Large, gold or silver metallic, feathered like a bird, eyes glow the same color as feathers.

Demeanor Passive unless a human is greedy.

Supernatural Powers Eats gold and silver. Feathers glow at night with the same hue as the precious metal they eat.

Location The hills and caves of the Atacama Desert, Chile.

Notes Seeing an Alicanto brings good luck, and legend says they will sometimes lead people to treasure. Humans are expected to share, or they may be pushed over a cliff. If this bird eats too much, it will be too heavy to fly. Some report a copper-eating Alicanto that is green in color.

BAGGE'S BLACK BIRD

Wingspan Unknown.

Physical Description As big as a sheep, black in color, call sounds like a bull.

Location Lake Bujuku, Uganda, East Africa.

Note Recorded by Stephen Bagge in 1898.

BAT BEAST OF KENT

Wingspan Very large; no exact size reported.

Physical Description Headless bat; approximately five feet tall; large, webbed feet; bat-like wings.

Demeanor Erratic and wobbly in its movements but not threatening.

Supernatural Powers Witnesses have reported seeing a glowing orb that floats overhead and then lands nearby.

Location County of Kent, Southeast England.

Notes Spotted in 1963 by four British teens and another, separate witness; appears to prefer staying hidden in the woods. Twenty-four-inch-long and nine-inch-wide footprints were found at the time of the sighting, along with flattened grass and foliage. Approximately two weeks later, the media investigated. While they saw no creature, they noted a soft glow permeating the area. The press caught the attention of a ufologist, who investigated and wrote the event off as a crow oddly illuminated by the flashing of an electric train passing not far away in the chilled autumnal air.[1]

CHICKCHARNEY

Wingspan Flightless.

Physical Description Face of an owl; three feet tall; covered in feathers but looks furry; has three fingers, three toes, and a monkey-like tail.

Demeanor Impish, mischievous. Bahamian folklore suggests these birds roam the deep forest underbrush. Make nests by joining two pine trees at the top.

Supernatural Powers Able to grant good or bad luck.

Location Andros Island, Bahamas.

Notes Chickcharney will grant good luck if you treat it nicely; if you laugh at the creature or the legend, it will curse you with the worst kind of misery.

Thought to be a close relative of *Tytos pollens*, a three-foot, flightless barn owl that went extinct after forests were destroyed in the late sixteenth and early seventeenth centuries.

CUÉLEBRE

Wingspan Bat-like wings with no designated size, but very large.

Physical Description Serpent-dragon covered with scales so thick they repel swords, arrows, or bullets; needle-like teeth; foul and poisonous breath.

Demeanor The Cuélebre comes out of its lair to wreak havoc on villagers by destroying their farms and fishing equipment, poisoning wells and springs, and demanding the sacrifice of herd animals and human virgins.

Supernatural Powers Able to spit fire. Some say its spit can turn into a magic stone with healing properties.

Location Asturia, in central northern Spain, situated between the Atlantic coast and the Cantabrian Mountains.

Notes The Cuélebre is said to live in a cave and guard his treasure. On midsummer night the dragon's magical spells are powerless, and men can defeat the dragon. But on Saint Bartholomew's Day, the serpent grows stronger and exacts revenge on those who have taken advantage of him. Although he is immortal, as he grows older, his scales grow thicker and harder and he must leave Asturia and fly to the Mar Cuajada, a paradise of immense treasure located beyond the sea.[2]

Hō-ō

Wingspan Unknown.

Physical Description Giant bird with a black beak and spotted black and red feathers. It has a single red stripe going down the middle of its back. Sleek, aerodynamic build.

Demeanor Passive, non-violent.

Location Japan and China.

Notes The name means "firebird," and this creature is also known as the Japanese phoenix. The bird's caw is a mix between an eagle and hawk. According to Chinese legend, the Hō-ō only appears to mark the beginning of a new era. At that time, it will descend from Heaven, bringing goodness to the Earth.

KIKIYAON, AKA SOUL CANNIBAL

Wingspan Large, but not specified. Feathered wings grow from its back.

Physical Description Five-foot-tall, owllike humanoid with a huge beak and greenish-grey hair. Spikes poke out of the back of its neck; talons on its large wings and feet; shoulders comes to a sharp point and can be used as weapons; carries a rotting smell.

Supernatural Powers Can outrun a man.

Demeanor Lies in wait to ambush travelers.

Location Africa; keeps to the forest.

Notes According to legend, a person who sees the Kikiyaoan will either die of shock or an illness.

KONGAMATO

Wingspan Some reports state three to four feet; others ten to twelve feet.

Physical Description Looks like a pterosaur with leathery red skin, black body, and brownish-red, bat-like wings; two-inch-long teeth stick out from lower jaw. Some report a doglike muzzle and long tail.

Demeanor Likes to glide between hilltops. Will swoop and attack humans.

Location Southwest Africa: Angola, Nambia, Zambia, and Congo.

Notes Kongamato means "breaker of boats." May also be referred to as Olitiau or Sasabonsam.[3] Frank H. Melland (*In Witchbound Africa*, 1923) showed locals pictures of *Pteranodons* which they confirmed

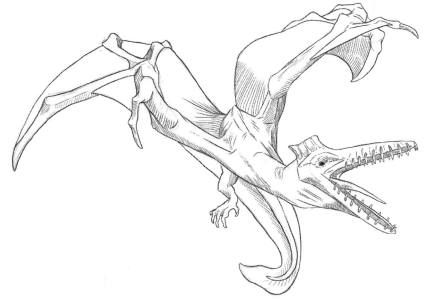

looked like the Kongamato. In 1988, an American who had been working with a team from the University of Chicago saw what he called "a giant black glider with white markings."[4]

La Lechuza

Physical Description Large, owllike body with the face of a woman. Makes the sound of a whistle or crying baby.

Demeanor Fiercely evil and dangerous. Waits for an unsuspecting victim to look at her, then attacks and scratches their eyes out.

Supernatural Powers Shapeshifter. Very strong. Can carry a full-grown man in her talons. Has the power to control the weather and can manipulate car batteries.

Location Texas and Mexico.

Notes Legend tells of a woman who sold her soul to the devil for shapeshifting powers. She appears as a woman during the day but shapeshifts into a large bird at night. If you hear the cry of La Lechuza it means she is about to make you her meal or someone in your family is going to die. Bullets cannot harm her, but you can protect yourself by using salt.

Manta-Man

Wingspan Large, leathery wings shaped like manta ray fins connect to the creature's body.

Physical Description Six-foot-tall humanoid with four limbs and spiky hair.

Demeanor Vicious toward animals.

Location Northern Chile.

Notes In 2013, there were several eyewitnesses in Bustamante Park. One couple reported they saw the figure perched in a church steeple. In pop culture, Manta Man is a character in the game *Fallout 4*.

MOUNT KANCING DRAGON

Wingspan Two wings. Very large but exact size unknown.

Physical Description Serpent body with head similar to a horse; four appendages in addition to wings.

Demeanor Terrorizes local villages; abducts and eats small children.

Location Lampung, Indonesia. Lives in underground caves.

Notes Ular Kuda means "horse serpent." While the existence of this cryptid is questionable, we were fond of the possibility and wondered what it might look like if it existed.

NAMIBIAN FLYING SNAKE

Wingspan Thirty feet.

Physical Description Nine to twenty-five feet long; yellowish-brown scales; serpentlike dragon with spots; bioluminescent crest and horns; bat-like wings; smells like tar.

Demeanor Can emit a loud roar that sounds like wind blowing through a pipe. Attacks livestock.

Supernatural Powers Can camouflage itself by changing color.

Location Namibia in the !Karas region. Namibia is the second least populated country in the world, consisting mostly of small livestock farmers.

Note In order to take off in flight, it hurls itself downhill.

One eyewitness account tells of a farmer who heard one of his cows bellowing in what sounded like pain. He went to check on it and saw what looked like a dragon. "It had a white bright light on its head, which was blinding me . . . it was brown and yellow . . . there was a tar-like smell coming from it, and it had smoke coming out of its nostrils."[5]

Orang-Bati

Physical Description Five-foot-tall winged primate with red skin, black leathery wings, and a long tail.

Demeanor Vicious. Will raid villages and abduct children. Emits long, mournful wail while on the prowl.

Location Island of Seram, Indonesia, which is the second largest island in Maluku Province. Lives in caves near the top of Mount Kairatu.

Notes Orang-Bati translates to "man with wings" or "man-bat." In 1987, an English missionary listened to many stories of the "man bat" that comes at night. Living in proximity to the Ropen, the Orang-bati might be the same pterosaur-type creature.

OWLMAN

Wingspan No designated size. Eyewitnesses say they are large, with long feathers.

Physical Description Five-foot-tall, owllike humanoid with greyish brown feathers, pointed horns, and red eyes; long legs with three-toed talons that some say look like pincers.

Demeanor Often reveals itself to young women. Not aggressive. Some believe it is territorial since all encounters take place around the same church.

Location Cornwall, England.

Notes Since 1976, people in the village of Mawnan have been reporting sightings in the forest surrounding a nearby church.

ROC

Wingspan Forty-eight feet.

Physical Description Gigantic white eagle.

Demeanor Aggressive. Described as a raptor / bird of prey.

Supernatural Powers Incredible strength.

Location Middle East and Africa.

Notes British historian, Rudolf Whittkower, identifies the Roc as the giant bird who carried off an elephant in the Middle Eastern myth titled, "The Bird and the Serpent." This may have some bearing on what Marco Polo recorded in his writings:

> 'Tis said that in those other Islands to the south, which the ships are unable to visit because this strong current prevents their return, is found the bird Gryphon, which appears there at certain seasons. The description given of it

is however entirely different from what our stories and pictures make it. For persons who had been there and had seen it told Messer Marco Polo that it was for all the world like an eagle, but one indeed of enormous size; so big in fact that its wings covered an extent of 30 paces, and its quills were 12 paces long, and thick in proportion. And it is so strong that it will seize an elephant in its talons and carry him high into the air, and drop him so that he is smashed to pieces; having so killed him the bird gryphon swoops down on him and eats him at leisure. The people of those isles call the bird Ruc, and it has no other name. So I wot not if this be the real gryphon, or if there be another manner of bird as great. But this I can tell you for certain, that they are not half lion and half bird as our stories do relate; but enormous as they be they are fashioned just like an eagle.[6]

Ropen

Two species have been reported in Papua New Guinea.

Wingspan Three to four feet for smaller species; twelve to fifteen feet for larger species.

Physical Description Mix between bat and pterosaur; dark grey skin; featherless; long, thin neck; crest on head; long beak with sharp teeth. Both species have a long skinny tail with a diamond-shaped flange on the tip and sharp talons.

Demeanor Typically stay deep in the jungle; only visible at night, when they give off a bioluminescent glow. Locals report that in the past these creatures were violent and would attack villages. They've since been hunted and stay far away. Prefer to be near water sources, where they feast on fish.

Locations Umboi Island, Papua New Guinea; Guantanamo Bay; Southern California; Texas.

Notes Giant clams have been found upstream in the jungle where Ropens are said to nest. The cryptids have also been accused of digging up graves to eat human flesh. This was during a time when dead bodies were customarily buried under loose dirt and leaves.

The flying cryptid, Kor, is thought to be similar to the Ropen.

SPRING-HEELED JACK

Physical Description Tall, lean, pale humanoid with a goatee beard; large, pointy ears; and a crow-like nose; glowing red eyes; metallic, talon-like claws. Wears tight white clothing with a black cape and helmet. Some have reported cloven hoofprints on rooftops where Spring-Heeled Jack was seen.

Demeanor Menacing, diabolical.

Supernatural Powers Fast. Has the ability to travel great distances in a single bound. Breathes out a bluish flame.

First Sighting 1837. Attacked a young woman, ripped at her clothes, and kissed her. When she cried for help, he left.

Location England, in and around London and the Black Country.

Notes Many sightings and attacks happen around pubs like the Dragon in the London district of Blackheath, the Swan in Whiteheath, the Wheatsheaf at Lye Cross, and the Lion in Tividale. Rumors have spread that wherever there were hoofprints, death soon followed.

Imitating Spring-Heeled Jack became a national craze in the early twentieth century. On one account, police arrested a man in the middle of the night who was wearing a miner's hat while jumping near the canal. The young man, Joseph Darby, explained he was training to become the World Spring Jumping Champion. He earned this title by beating an American, W. G. Hamlington, in 1887.

The last documented reports of Spring Heeled Jack were in Liverpool in 1904 and Bradford in 1926.

WAKWAK

Wingspan Unknown.

Physical Description Bat-like, with long, sharp, black talons.

Demeanor Vicious. Slashes victims wide open to feed on their heart.

Supernatural Powers Some believe Wakwak is a cryptid that belongs to a witch, others believe it can shapeshift into a vampire.

Location Philippines.

Notes In Philippine lore the Wakwak is one form a vampire can take. It is closely related to the Aswang, which has a human body and face, long claws and teeth, and long, bat-like wings. Both cryptids can shape-shift. Legend states the Wakwak snatches humans from their beds at night. The Wakwak gets its name from the noises it makes when it flaps its wings. If you can hear the flapping sound it means the creature is far way. The closer it gets to prey, the quieter it will be.

NOTES

1. What Are Sky Monsters?

1. Ross Piper, *Extinct Animals: An Encyclopedia of Animals That Have Disappeared During Human History* (Westport, CT: Greenwood Press, 2009), 121.
2. For sightings of giant, plane-sized birds near the Olympic Peninsula in Oregon and in Walnut, California, see Mark A. Hall, *Thunderbirds: America's Living Legends of Giant Birds.* (New York: Cosimo Classic, 2007), 71, 72.
3. Hall, *Thunderbirds*, 110.
4. W. F. Mayer, "In the Pines," *Atlantic Monthly* 3 (May 1859): 560–69.
5. "The Engineer Quit His Run," *The New York Sun,* January 22, 1893, p. 6. https://chroniclingamerica.loc.gov/lccn/sn83030272/1893-01-22/ed-1/seq-18/#date1=1893&index=1&rows=20&words=Devil+Leeds&searchType=basic&sequence=0&state=&date2=1893&proxtext=Leeds+Devil&y=16&x=24&dateFilterType=yearRange&page=1.
6. Brian Regal and Frank Esposito, *The Secret History of the Jersey Devil* (Baltimore, MD: John Hopkins University Press): 86. The authors discuss the John Elfreth Watkins article, "Demon of the Pines," Washington, DC, Evening Star (September 2, 1905).
7. Stories recounted in James F. McCloy and Ray Miller Jr.'s *The Jersey Devil* (Indianapolis, IN: Blue River Press, 2016) without original sources.
8. Henry Charleton Beck, *Jersey Genesis: Story of the Mullica River* (Rutgers, NJ: Rutgers University Press, 1983).
9. John Keel, *The Mothman Prophecies* (New York: Saturday Review Press, 1975), 78.
10. Donnie Sergent Jr. and Jeff Wamsley, *Mothman: The Facts Behind the Legend* (Point Pleasant, WV: Mothman Lives Publishing, 2020), 20.
11. Ted Slowik, "Chicago's 'Mothman' Stories Are Good Paranormal Entertainment," *Chicago Tribune*, Daily Southtown, July 29, 2017, https://www.chicagotribune.com/suburbs/daily-southtown/opinion/ct-sta-slowik-chicago-mothman-st-0730-20170728-story.html.

2. Who's Who in the American Sky?

1. Ken Gerhard, *Big Bird! Modern Sightings of Flying Monsters* (Woosery, UK: CFZ Press, 2007), 19–21.
2. Jason Offutt, *Chasing American Monsters* (Woodbury, MN: Llewellyn Publications, 2019), 92.
3. *New York Times*, "An Aerial Mystery," September 12, 1880, https://www.nytimes.com/1880/09/12/archives/an-aerial-mystery.html.
4. Ken Gerhard, *Encounters with Flying Humanoids: Mothman, Manbirds, Gargoyles, and Other Winged Beasts* (Woodbury, MN: Llewellyn Publications, 2013), 183.

3. History and Legends

1. Mann's comments appear in Adrienne Mayor's *Fossil Legends of the First Americans* (Princeton, NJ: Princeton University Press, 2005), 29.

2. Mayor, *Fossil Legends,* 104. Teratorn remains have been found across the southern United States (and recently in Oregon) and northern Mexico.

3. This version of the story is a summary of Anne Siberell's children's book *Whale in the Sky* (London: Puffin, 1985).

4. University of Nebraska Press / University of Nebraska-Lincoln Libraries-Electronic Text Center, *The Journals of the Lewis and Clark Expedition,* "Clark: August 30, 1803," https://lewisandclarkjournals.unl.edu/item/lc.jrn.1805-10-31.

5. Darlene Geis's *Dinosaurs and Other Prehistoric Animals* (New York: Grosset & Dunlap, 1972), 9–10. The author does not give a source for this story. We find the story in other locations, also with unknown origin. We have corrected style and grammar, but the content of the story remains intact.

6. Thomas Jefferson, *The Complete Works of Thomas Jefferson: Autobiography, Correspondence, Reports, Messages, Speeches and Other Official and Private Writings* (Prague, CZE: e-artnow, 2018).

7. Adapted from Aurora Conley, "How the Birch Tree Got It's Burns: An Ojibwe Legend Retold," *Using Native American Legends to Teach Mathematics,* UW Oshkosh, accessed August 2019, http://www.uwosh.edu/coehs/cmagproject/ethnomath/legend/legend10.htm.

8. *Indigenous Peoples Literature,* "Passamaquoddy Nation," July 30, 2017, https://indigenouspeoplenet.wordpress.com/2017/01/30/passamaquoddy-literature/.

9. *Indigenous Peoples Literature,* "Passamaquoddy Nation."

10. This is a summary of Beatrice Orcutt Harrell's children's book *How Thunder and Lightning Came to Be* (New York: Dial Books for Young Readers, 1995).

11. R. W. Giddings, "Yaqui Myths and Legends" in *Anthropological Papers of the University of Arizona* (Tucson: University of Arizona Press, 1959), 36–38.

12. Mayor, *Fossil Legends,* 165.

13. Johan De Laet, 1625–1640, "From the 'New World,'" in *Narratives of New Netherland, 1609–1664: Volume 8,* ed. John Franklin Jameson (Bedford, MA: Applewood Books, 1909), 57, https://www.google.com/books/edition/Narratives_of_New_Netherland/j1sKi0KPTewC?hl=en&gbpv=1&dq=Google+Books+Narratives+of+New+Netherland,+1609–1664,&printsec=frontcover.

14. Digital History. "Persecution of the Quakers." Accessed August 2018. https://www.digitalhistory.uh.edu/disp_textbook.cfm?smtID=3&psid=94#:~:text=In%201660%2C%20Edward%20Burrough%20catalogued,three%20Quakers%20had%20been%20executed.

15. Benjamin Franklin, "Poor Richard, 1733," *Founders Online,* National Archives, https://founders.archives.gov/documents/Franklin/01-01-02-0093.

16. Karen B. Riley, *The Pine Barrens of New Jersey* (Charleston: Arcadia, 2010), 38.

17. Kwame Dakwa, "The Kallikak Family: Goddard's Regrets," Human Intelligence, Fall 2001, https://www.intelltheory.com/kallikak.shtml, citing Leila Zenderland's *Measuring Minds: Henry Herbert Goddard and the Origins of American Intelligence Testing* (Cambridge, UK: Cambridge University Press, 1998), 324–26.

18. Colin G. Calloway, *The Shawnees and the War for America* (New York: Viking Penguin Group, 2007), 479.

19. John Stuart, *Memoir of the Indian Wars* (1763), United States History Commons and History at DigitalCommons@Providence, *Primary Sources*, Paper 6. https://digitalcommons .providence.edu/cgi/viewcontent.cgi?article=1005&context=primary, 49.

20. Calloway, *The Shawnees*, 729.

21. Calloway, *The Shawnees*, 748.

22. George Roche, *The Book of Heroes: Great Men and Women in American History: Volume 1.* (Washington D.C.: Regnery Publishing Inc., 1998), 52.

23. Stuart, *Memoir*, 48. Stuart's quoted materials were originally recorded in a compilation edited by his brother: John Stuart, 1799, *Memoir of Indian Wars and Other Occurrences by the Late Colonel Stuart of Greenbrier: Eyewitness Accounts of the American Revolution Series,* edited by Charles A. Stuart (Salem, NH: Ayers Company Publishers, 1970).

24. Chris Rizer, "Mason County Memories: A Curse Upon the Land," *Point Pleasant Register*, October 27, 2018. https://www.mydailyregister.com/news/33706/mason-county -memories-a-curse-upon-the-land.

25. Stuart, *Memoir*, 62.

4. Sky Monster Culture

1. Wicasta Lovelace, "Introduction to the Online Edition," *Malleus Maleficarum of Heinrich Kramer and James Sprenger,* trans. Reverend Montague Summers (Mineola, NY: Dover, 1948), http://www.malleusmaleficarum.org.

2. The quote and history can be found at "Point Pleasant Depot," n.d., GlobalSecurity .org, accessed August 2019, https://www.globalsecurity.org/military/facility/point-pleasant .htm.

3. Orwell's column for the *Tribune* is available through the Orwell Foundation: "You and the Atomic Bomb," *Tribune*, October 19, 1945, https://www.orwellfoundation.com/the-orwell -foundation/orwell/essays-and-other-works/you-and-the-atom-bomb/.

4. Quoted in Megan Garber, "The Man Who Introduced the World to Flying Saucers," *Atlantic*, Technology, June 15, 2014, https://www.theatlantic.com/technology/archive/2014/06 /the-man-who-introduced-the-world-to-flying-saucers/372732/.

5. Full details on this project can be found at the United States Environmental Protection Agency, "West Virginia Ordinance (US Army) Point Pleasant, WV," accessed September 2019, https://cumulis.epa.gov/supercpad/SiteProfiles/index.cfm?fuseaction=second.cleanup &id=0303066.

6. Anthony DeStefano, *The Invisible World* (New York: Doubleday, 2011), 14.

7. Charles Lindbergh, quoted in "Charles Lindbergh Biography," CharlesLindbergh.com, accessed November 4, 2019, http://www.charleslindbergh.com/history/index.asp.

8. Gordon Russell Young, *The Army Almanac: A Book of Facts Concerning the United States Army* (Harrisburg, PA: The Stackpole Company, 1959).

9. U.S. Air Force, "Thunderbirds," April 25, 2003, https://www.af.mil/About-Us/Fact -Sheets/Display/Article/104552/thunderbirds/.

10. Mod Betty, "The Original Thunderbird, Broomall, PA," Retro Road Map, November 7, 2015, http://www.retroroadmap.com/spot/the-original-thunderbird-broomall-pa -cheesesteaks-hoagies-and-pizza-since-1956/.

11. Quote is from Maria Panaritis, "As the Eagles Fly, So Does Thunderbird, the Delco Steak Shop That Is All Fight and Heart," *Philadelphia Inquirer*, January 4, 2019. https://www

.inquirer.com/news/columnists/eagles-bears-delaware-county-broomall-thunderbird -cheesesteaks-diner-nfl-playoffs-maria-panaritis-20190104.html.

12. SeattleThunderbirds.com, "About," accessed September 2019, https:// seattlethunderbirds.com/pages-team-about.

13. Lawrie Mifflin and Michael Katz, "'Jersey Devils' Wins Name Poll," *New York Times*, Scouting, June 30, 1982, https://www.nytimes.com/1982/06/30/sports/scouting-jersey-devils -wins-name-poll.html.

5. Fact or Fiction?

1. Cryptid Wiki, "Lone Pine Mountain Devil," accessed October 2019, https://cryptidz .fandom.com/wiki/Lone_Pine_Mountain_Devil.

2. Niki Wilson, "The Reign of the Terror Birds," *BBC Earth*, July 24, 2015, http://www .bbc.com/earth/story/20150727-the-reign-of-the-terror-birds.

3. James Gregory, "California Migration History 1850–2017," America's Great Migration Project, University of Washington, https://depts.washington.edu/moving1/California.shtml.

4. Chandra Johnson, *Deseret News*, updated October 23, 2014, https://www.deseret.com /2014/10/23/20551054/what-scary-stories-have-in-common-with-religion.

5. McCloy and Miller, *The Jersey Devil*, 45.

6. Joseph A. Gambardello, "The Jersey Devil, the Tale of a Viral Story from 110 Years Ago," *The Philadelphia Inquirer*, updated January 23, 2019, https://www.inquirer.com/news /new-jersey/jersey-devil-history-fake-news-norman-jeffries-20190123.html.

7. Gambardello, "The Jersey Devil."

8. Gary Small, "Mass Hysteria Can Strike Anywhere, Anytime," *Psychology Today*, September 28, 2010, https://www.psychologytoday.com/us/blog/brain-bootcamp/201009/mass -hysteria-can-strike-anywhere-anytime.

9. Digitally archived by the Wisconsin Historical Society at AmericanJourneys.org. Jacques Marquette, *The Mississippi Voyage of Jolliet and Marquette, 1673* (Madison: Wisconsin Historical Society, 2003), 248–49. https://www.americanjourneys.org/pdf/AJ-051.pdf. Jacques Marquette was originally quoted in Reuben Gold Thwaites, ed., *The Jesuit Relations and Allied Documents* (Cleveland: 1896–1901), LIX, 97.

10. John Russell, "The Piasa: An Indian Tradition of Illinois." *Family Magazine, or, Monthly Abstract of General Knowledge*, vol. 4, 101, 1836.

11. From Paul Nation's blog "The Invada Bird Project," accessed October 31, 2019, https:// indavabird.com/.

12. Pterosaurs Still Living. "An American Soldier Sees a Pteradactyl." Accessed October 2019. http://www.laattorneyvideo.com/nonlegal/pterosaurs/DH/

13. Pterosaurs Still Living. "Whitcomb Expedition of 2004." Accessed October 2019. http://www.laattorneyvideo.com/nonlegal/pterosaurs/news-rel/.

14. Wikipedia, "Papua New Guinea," updated September 15, 2020, https://en.wikipedia .org/wiki/New_Guinea_campaign.

15. Milt Macy, "Pterodactyl Caught on Camera. Part Two," accessed October 2019, https:// www.youtube.com/watch?v=Ws11DaRsbjI. A partial transcript of the interview can be found at Jonathan Whitcomb, *Live Pterosaur*, "Modern Living Pterosaur in a Remote Jungle in Papua New Guinea," August 23, 2018, https://www.livepterosaur.com/LP_Blog/archives/9545.

16. Alex Lickerman, "What Do You Want?" *Psychology Today*, August 5, 2012, https://www.psychologytoday.com/us/blog/happiness-in-world/201208/what-do-you-want.

6. Who's Who in the Sky around the World?

1. High Strangeness, "Bat Beast of Kent," accessed October 2019, https://high-strangeness.fandom.com/wiki/Bat_Beast_of_Kent#cite_note-1.
2. Everything Dragon Shop, "The Cuélebre," accessed October 2019, https://www.everythingdragonshop.com/dragon-articles/dragon-mythology-the-cuelebre/.
3. See Loren Coleman and Jerome Clark, *Cryptozoology A to Z: The Encyclopedia of Loch Monsters, Sasquatch, Chupacabras, and other Authentic Mysteries of Nature* (New York: Fireside, 1999) for an explanation of why these names may be synonymous with the Kongamato.
4. Coleman and Clark, *Cryptozoology A to Z*.
5. Fandom, "Namibian Flying Snakes," accessed October 2019, https://cryptidarchives.fandom.com/wiki/Namibian_flying_snake.
6. *The Travels of Marco Polo*, Book 3, Chapter 33, "Concerning the Island of Madeigascar," accessed October 2020, https://en.wikisource.org/wiki/The_Travels_of_Marco_Polo/Book_3/Chapter_33.

SOURCES AND FURTHER READING

Albarelli, H. P., Jr. "Has the Awful Returned to Berkshire & Richford?" *Lovecraft and His Legacy* (blog). October 19, 2006. http://chrisperridas.blogspot.com/2006/10/lovecrafts -cryptid-awful.html.

American Indians Heritage Foundation / Indians.org. *Indigenous Peoples' Literature.* "Chinook Creation Story." Accessed August 2019. http://www.indians.org/welker/chinook .htm.

Atlas Obscura. "Meet Spring-Heeled Jack, the Leaping Devil That Terrorized Victorian England." October 6, 2016. https://www.atlasobscura.com/articles/meet-springheeled -jack-the-leaping-devil-that-terrorized-victorian-england.

Beck, Henry Charlton. *Jersey Genesis: The Story of the Mullica River.* New Brunswick, NJ: Rutgers University Press, 1963.

Bielawa, Michael J. "Bridgeport's UFO Legacy: Men in Black and the Albert K. Bender Story." Bielawa Bridgeport Library. Accessed August 2019. https://bportlibrary.org/hc /authors/bridgeports-ufo-legacy-men-in-black-and-the-albert-k-bender-story.

Blumberg, Jess. "A Brief History of the Salem Witch Trials." *Smithsonian Magazine,* Ask Smithsonian, October 23, 2007. https://www.smithsonianmag.com/history/a-brief -history-of-the-salem-witch-trials-175162489.

Bolte, Jason. *Point Pleasant.* Charleston, SC: Arcadia Publishing, 2007.

Calloway, Colin G. *The Shawnees and the War for America.* New York: Viking Penguin Group, 2007.

Charles Lindbergh.com. "Charles Lindbergh Biography." Accessed November 4, 2019. http:// www.charleslindbergh.com/history/index.asp.

Cheeseman, Evelyn. *The Two Roads of Papua.* London: Jarrold's, 1935.

Clark, William. "October 31, 1805." Journals of the Lewis and Clark Expedition. Accessed August 2019. https://lewisandclarkjournals.unl.edu/item/lc.jrn.1805-10-31.

Coleman, Loren. *Mothman Evil Incarnate: The Unauthorized Companion to the Mothman Prophecies.* New York: Cosimo Books, 2017.

Coleman, Loren, and Clark, Jerome. *Cryptozoology A to Z.* New York: Simon & Schuster, 1999.

Conley, Aurora. "How the Birch Tree Got It's [sic] Burns, an Ojibwe Legend Retold." Closing the Math Achievement Gap. University of Wisconsin Oshkosh. Accessed August 2019. http://www.uwosh.edu/coehs/cmagproject/ethnomath/legend/legend10.htm.

Cryptid Wiki. "Achiyalabopa." Accessed November 11, 2019. https://cryptidz.fandom.com /wiki/Achiyalabopa

Cryptid Wiki. "Bat Beast of Kent." Accessed November 13, 2019. https://cryptidz.fandom.com /wiki/Bat_Beast_of_Kent.

Cryptid Wiki. "Lone Pine Mountain Devil." Accessed October 2019. https://cryptidz.fandom .com/wiki/Lone_Pine_Mountain_Devil.

De Laet, Johan. "From the New World." In *Narratives of New Netherland, 1609–1664.* Edited by John Franklin Jameson, 29–60. Vol. 8 of *Original Narratives of Early American His-*

tory. Bedford, MA: Applewood Books, 1909. https://www.google.com/books/edition
/Narratives_of_New_Netherland/j1sKioKPTewC?hl=en&gbpv=1&dq=Google+Books
+Narratives+of+New+Netherland,+1609–1664,&printsec=frontcover.

Dennett, Andrea Stulman. *Weird and Wonderful: The Dime Museum in America*. New York:
New York University Press, 1997.

DeStefano, Anthony. *The Invisible World*. New York: Doubleday, 2011.

Digital History. "Persecution of the Quakers." Accessed August 2019. https://www.digital
history.uh.edu/disp_textbook.cfm?smtID=3&psid=94#:~:text=In%201660%2C
%20Edward%20Burrough%20catalogued,three%20Quakers%20had%20been
%20executed.

Everhart, Michael J. *Oceans of Kansas*, 2nd ed. Bloomington: Indiana University Press, 2017.

First People of America and Canada—Turtle Island. "American Indian Legends: The Bridge
of the Gods." Accessed August 2019. https://www.firstpeople.us/FP-Html-Legends/The
_Bridge_Of_The_Gods-Unknown.html.

Franklin, Benjamin. "Poor Richard, 1733." *Founders Online*, National Archives, https://found-
ers.archives.gov/documents/Franklin/01-01-02-0093. [Original source: *The Papers of
Benjamin Franklin*, vol. 1, *January 6, 1706 through December 31, 1734*, ed. Leonard W.
Labaree. New Haven: Yale University Press, 1959, pp. 280–318.]

Gambardello, Joseph A. "The Jersey Devil, the Tale of a Viral Story from 110 Years Ago."
Philadelphia Inquirer. Updated January 23, 2019. https://www.inquirer.com/news/new
-jersey/jersey-devil-history-fake-news-norman-jeffries-20190123.html.

Geis, Darlene. *Dinosaurs and Other Prehistoric Animals*. New York: Grosset & Dunlap, 1972.

Genesis Park. "The Ropen of Papua New Guinea." Accessed October 31, 2019. https://www
.genesispark.com/exhibits/evidence/cryptozoological/pterosaurs/ropen/.

GeoKansas. "Monument Rocks." Accessed August 2019. http://geokansas.ku.edu/monument
-rocks.

Gerhard, Ken. *Encounters with Flying Humanoids: Mothman, Manbirds, Gargoyles, and
Other Winged Beasts*. Woodbury, MN: Llewellyn Publications, 2016.

Giddings, Ruth Warner. "Yaqui Myths and Legends." *Anthropological Papers of the University
of Arizona* 2, 36–38. Tucson: University of Tucson, 1959.

Global Security.org. "Point Pleasant Depot." Accessed August 2019. https://www.global
security.org/military/facility/point-pleasant.htm.

Goddard, H. H. *The Kallikak Family: A Study in the Heredity of Feeble-Mindedness*. New
York: Macmillan, 1912.

Gregory, James. "California Migration History 1850–2017." America's Great Migration Project, University of Washington. https://depts.washington.edu/moving1/California
.shtml.

Habib, Mike. "Anatomy." Pterosaur.net. Accessed August 2019. https://pterosaur.net
/anatomy.php.

Hairr, John. *Monsters of North Carolina: Mysterious Creatures in the Tar Heel State*. Mechan-
icsburg, PA: Stackpole Books, 2003.

Hall, Mark. *Thunderbirds, America's Living Legends of Giant Birds*. New York: Cosimo Clas-
sics, 2007.

Harrell, Beatrice O. *How Thunder and Lightning Came to Be*. New York: Dial Books for
Young Readers, 1955.

Harvey, Henry. *History of the Shawnee Indians, from the Year 1681 to 1854, Inclusive*. Cincin-
nati: Ephraim Morgan and Sons, 1855.

High Strangeness. "Bat Beast of Kent." Accessed October 2019. https://high-strangeness
.fandom.com/wiki/Bat_Beast_of_Kent#cite_note-1.

History.com. "History of UFO's." October 27, 2009. Updated September 11, 2019. https://
www.history.com/topics/paranormal/history-of-ufos.

Indigenous Peoples Literature. Passamaquoddy Nation. July 30, 2017 https://indigenous
peoplenet.wordpress.com/2017/01/30/passamaquoddy-literature/.

Jefferson, Thomas. 1743–1826. Edited by Albert Ellery Bergh, Andrew Adgate Lipscomb, and
Thomas Jefferson Memorial Association of the United States. *The Writings of Thomas
Jefferson*, Library ed., containing his Autobiography, Notes on Virginia, parliamentary
manual, official papers, messages and addresses, and other writings [. . .]. Washington,
D.C.: Issued under the auspices of the Thomas Jefferson memorial association of the
United States, 1903–4.

Jefferson, Thomas. *The Complete Works of Thomas Jefferson: Autobiography, Correspondence,
Reports, Messages, Speeches and Other Official and Private Writings.* Prague, CZE:
e-artnow, 2018. https://books.google.com/books?id=YoljDwAAQBAJ.

Johnson, Chandra. "What Scary Stories Have in Common with Religion." *Deseret News.*
October 23, 2014. https://www.deseret.com/2014/10/23/20551054/what-scary-stories
-have-in-common-with-religion.

Keel, John A. *Mothman Prophecies.* New York: Tor Books, 1991.

Kramer, Heinrich, and James Sprenger. *The Malleus Maleficarum.* Translated by Montague
Summers. Unabridged online reproduction of the 1928 edition. 2002. http://www
.malleusmaleficarum.org.

Kwakiutl Band Council. "Our Culture: Kwakiutl in Fort Rupert: A Short History." Accessed
August 2019. http://www.kwakiutl.bc.ca/Our-Culture.

Landis, Don, ed., with Jackson Hole Bible College. *The Secrets of Ancient Man: Revelations
from the Ruins.* Green Forest, AR: Master Books, 2015.

Legends of America. "Native American Religion." Accessed August 2019. https://www
.legendsofamerica.com/na-religion.

Lewis, C. S. 1941. *The Screwtape Letters: Letters from a Senior to a Junior Devil.* Québec, CA:
Samizdat University Press. 2016. http://www.samizdat.qc.ca/arts/lit/PDFs/Screwtape
Letters_CSL.pdf.

Lickerman, Alex. *The Undefeated Mind: Constructing an Indestructible Self.* Boca Raton, FL:
Health Communications Inc., 2012.

Lickerman, Alex. "What Do You Want?" *Psychology Today*, August 5, 2012. https://www
.psychologytoday.com/us/blog/happiness-in-world/201208/what-do-you-want.

Macfarlan, Alan A. *North American Indian Legends.* Mineola, NY: Dover Publications, 1968.

Madriga, Emily. "17 Creepy Facts about the Lechuza." *Thought Catalog*, August 10, 2018.
https://thoughtcatalog.com/emily-madriga/2018/03/17-facts-about-the-lechuza-and
-lechuza-stories/.

Manje, Juan Mateo. *Unknown Arizona and Sonora 1693–1721 from the Francisco Fernandez
Del Castillo Version of Luz De Tierra Incognita.* Tucson: Arizona Silhouettes, 1954.

Manno, Nina. s.v. "Benjamin Bonneville (1796–1878)." In *The Oregon Encyclopedia.* Accessed
March 2019. https://oregonencyclopedia.org/articles/bonneville_benjamin/.

Marquette, Jacques. "The Mississippi Voyage of Jolliet and Marquette, 1673." Madison: Wisconsin Historical Society, 2003. https://www.americanjourneys.org/pdf/AJ-051.pdf.

Mayer, W. F. "In the Pines." *Atlantic Monthly* 3 (May 1859): 560–69.

Mayor, Adrienne. *Fossil Legends of the First Americans*. Princeton, NJ: Princeton University Press, 2005.

McCloy, James F., and Ray Miller Jr. *The Jersey Devil*. Moorestown, NJ: Middle Atlantic Press, 2005.

Mifflin, Lawrie. "Jersey Devils Wins Name Poll." *New York Times*. June 30, 1982. https://www.nytimes.com/1982/06/30/sports/scouting-jersey-devils-wins-name-poll.html ?searchResultPosition=1.

Mullins, G. W. *Walking with Spirits*. Vol. 2, *Native American Myths, Legends, and Folklore*. Carbondale, CO: Light of the Moon Publishing, 2019.

Myers, Jeff. *The Secret Battle of Ideas About God*. Colorado Springs, CO: David C. Cook, 2017.

Myss, Caroline. "Native American Spirituality." Myss.com. Accessed August 2019. https://www.myss.com/free-resources/world-religions/native-american-spirituality.

Nation, Paul. "Indava Bird Project." Accessed October 31, 2019. https://indavabird.com/.

Native American Indian Facts. "Totem Pole Facts." Accessed August 2019. https://native -american-indian-facts.com/Native-American-Indian-Art-Facts/Native-American -Indian-Totem-Pole-Facts.html.

New England Historical Society. N.d. Updated, 2020. "The Deadly Rules of Massachusetts' Court of Oyer and Terminer." http://www.newenglandhistoricalsociety.com/rules -massachusetts-court-of-oyer-and-terminer.

Offutt, Jason. *Chasing American Monsters*. Woodbury, MN: Llewellyn Publications, 2019.

Oregon-California Trails Association. "Final Leg of the Oregon Trail." Accessed August 2019. https://www.octa-trails.org/articles/final-leg-of-the-oregon-trail/.

Orwell, George. 1945. "You and the Atom Bomb." *Tribune*, October 19, 1945. Repr. the Orwell Foundation. Accessed August 2019. https://www.orwellfoundation.com/the-orwell -foundation/orwell/essays-and-other-works/you-and-the-atom-bomb/.

Pedlow, Gregory W., and Donald E. Welzenbach. 1998. "The CIA and the U-2 Program 1954–1974." Central Intelligence Agency. https://www.cia.gov/library/center-for-the -study-of-intelligence/csi-publications/books-and-monographs/the-cia-and-the-u-2 -program-1954–1974/u2.pdf.

Piper, Ross. *Extinct Animals*. Westport, CT: Greenwood Press, 2009.

Port of Cascade Locks. "Bridge of the Gods." Accessed November 4, 2019. https://portof cascadelocks.org/bridge-of-the-gods/.

Public Service Commission of West Virginia. 1982. "Case No. 81–469-W-CN: City of Point Pleasant Application for a certificate of convenience and necessity for new water supply facilities." June 3, 2982. http://www.psc.state.wv.us/scripts/orders/ViewDocument.cfm ?CaseActivityID=13582&Source=Archives.

Regal, Brian, and Frank J. Esposito. *The Secret History of the Jersey Devil*. Baltimore, MD: John Hopkins University Press, 2018.

Riley, Karen R. *The Pine Barrens of New Jersey*. Charleston, SC: Arcadia Publishing, 2010.

Rizer, Chris. "The Marietta Manufacturing Company." *Point Pleasant Register*, June 14, 2019. https://www.mydailyregister.com/news/42102/the-marietta-manufacturing-company.

Rizer, Chris. "Mason County Memories: A Curse Upon the Land." Point Pleasant Register, October 27, 2018. https://www.mydailyregister.com/news/33706/mason-county -memories-a-curse-upon-the-land.

Roche, George. *The Book of Heroes: Great Men and Women in American History*, Vol. 1. Washington, DC: Regnery Publishing, 1998.

Russell, John. "The Piasa: An Indian Tradition of Illinois." *Family Magazine, or, Monthly Abstract of General Knowledge,* vol. 4, 101. New York: Redfield and Lindsay, 1836.

SeattleThunderbirds.com. "About." Accessed September 2019. https://seattlethunderbirds .com/pages-team-about.

Sergent, Donnie, Jr., and Jeff Wamsley. *Mothman: The Facts Behind the Legend.* Proctorville, OH: Mark S. Phillips Publishing, 2002.

Siberell, Anne. *Whale in the Sky.* London: Puffin, 1985.

Slowik, Ted. "Column: Chicago's 'Mothman' stories are good paranormal entertainment," *Chicago Tribune,* Daily Southtown, July 29, 2017. https://www.chicagotribune.com /suburbs/daily-southtown/opinion/ct-sta-slowik-chicago-mothman-st-0730-20170728 -story.html.

Small, Gary. "Mass Hysteria Can Strike Anywhere, Anytime." *Psychology Today,* September 28, 2010. https://www.psychologytoday.com/us/blog/brain-bootcamp/201009/mass -hysteria-can-strike-anywhere-anytime.

Solem-Stull, Barbara. *Ghost Towns and Other Quirky Places in the New Jersey Pine Barrens.* Medford, NJ: Plexus Publishing, 2005.

Sprouse, Bill. *The Domestic Life of the Jersey Devil or, Bebop's Miscellany.* Egg Harbor, NJ: Oyster Eye Publishing, 2013.

Strain, Kathy M. *Giants, Cannibals, and Monsters.* Blaine, WA: Hancock House Publishers, 2008.

Swancer, Brent. "Bizarre Encounters with Batsquatch." Mysterious Universe. June 7, 2018. https://mysteriousuniverse.org/2018/06/bizarre-encounters-with-the-batsquatch/.

Taylor, Troy. *Haunted Alton.* 4th ed. Decatur, IL: Whitechapel Press, 2014.

Temple, Wayne C. "The Piasa Bird: Fact or Fiction?" *Journal of the Illinois State Historical Society (1908–1984)* 49, no. 3 (Autumn 1956): 308–27.

The Travels of Marco Polo, Book 3, Chapter 33, "Concerning the Island of Madeigascar." Accessed October 2020, https://en.wikisource.org/wiki/The_Travels_of_Marco_Polo /Book_3/Chapter_33.

Trafzer, Clifford E. *The Chinook.* New York: Chelsea House Publishers, 1990.

United States Air Force. "Thunderbirds." April 25, 2003. https://www.af.mil/About-Us/Fact -Sheets/Display/Article/104552/thunderbirds/.

United States Environmental Protection Agency. "West Virginia Ordinance (US Army) Point Pleasant, WV." Accessed September 2019. https://cumulis.epa.gov/supercpad /SiteProfiles/index.cfm?fuseaction=second.cleanup&id=0303066.

Vecsey, Christopher. *Traditional Ojibwa Religion and Its Historical Changes,* 152: 75. American Philosophical Society, 1983.

Western Mining History. "California Mining Towns." Accessed 10/6/2020. https:// westernmininghistory.com/state/california/.

Whitcomb, Johnathan. *Pterosaurs Still Living* (blog). Accessed October 31, 2019. https:// laattorneyvideo.com/nonlegal/pterosaurs/.

Williams, Andrew, and Kyle Warmack. "Marietta Manufacturing Company." Clio: Your Guide to History. January 14, 2019. https://www.theclio.com/entry/8504.

Wilson, Niki. "The Reign of the Terror Birds." *BBC Earth,* July 24, 2015. http://www.bbc.com /earth/story/20150727-the-reign-of-the-terror-birds.

World Heritage Encyclopedia. s.v. "Quaker Act of 1622." Accessed August 2019. http://www .gutenberg.us/articles/quaker_act_1662.

Young, Gordon Russell. 1959. *The Army Almanac: A Book of Facts Concerning the United States Army*. Harrisburg, PA: The Stackpole Company. https://babel.hathitrust.org/cgi/pt?id=mdp.39015022444585&view=1up&seq=68.

Zenderland, Leila. 1998. *Measuring Minds: Henry Herbert Goddard and the Origins of American Intelligence Testing*. Cambridge, UK: Cambridge University Press.

INDEX

Page numbers in italics refer to illustrations

After graduating high school in 2014, MEL CABRE fine-tuned her passion for designing creatures, cryptids, and monsters by closely studying the world around her and teaching herself the basics of animal and human anatomy. Constant inspiration by the uniqueness found in nature keeps Mel's imagination alive. She is newly married to a man who rolls with all of her wacky thought processes and loves cats as much as she does.

T. S. MART specializes in writing true-to-life stories and showcasing ordinary people in extraordinary circumstances. Her short story "Delivering Hope" won first place in a national competition and appeared in a bestselling anthology. With a background in social work, she makes her home in a small midwestern town, where she writes to inspire and entertain. T. S. Mart is also the owner of Cryptid World, where she offers family-friendly content on cryptids, creatures, and fascinating creations.